M.A.D.* LEADERSHIP

*MAKE A DIFFERENCE

*Show the People Light and They
Will Find Their Way*

OMAR REID

To my wife, Janice, you are the glue to our family. Your love has allowed me to become the person I am.

To my daughter, Briana, keep walking into your destiny with greatness.

To my mother, Jessie, for being a marvelous inspiration and a God-given incredibly special someone who shaped who I am today.

Table of Contents

Introduction

Leadership is Your Ticket to Be M.A.D.
My Book Can Show You How

"What you do and act as a leader makes a difference, and you have to decide what kind... and how much of a difference you want to make."
– Omar Reid

During my leadership journey, I have learned many valuable lessons. From my first leadership experience back in middle school where I was elected president of the Sigma Beta Club and we learned Robert's Rules in the back of Maple Valley library in Akron, Ohio, to being the captain of Little League and high school and college sports teams, my lessons were direct and diverse and, most importantly, set the stage for what came later. I guess "Leadership DNA" was in my blood from an early age. I didn't quite realize that I wanted to be M.A.D. — Making A Difference — however small it might have been back then.

I can't remember a time when I wasn't in some type of leadership role from my first formal supervisory experience at UPS where I had six preloaders working for me, and we loaded 27 package trucks a night, to running the fourth largest overnight operation in the company where we processed over 140,000 packages per night. And I directed a corporate beta test facility in Southeast Houston, where I was responsible for advanced technology deployed across the enterprise.

Being on the boards of non-profits such as Communities In Schools, Big Brothers, Big Sisters, Center for Civic and Public Policy Improvement, and Fourth Ward Tax Increment Redevelopment Zone to name just a few, to leading in a fraternity Phi Beta Sigma and my church leadership at Wheeler Avenue Baptist, my leadership skills were tested and strengthened, and I learned how to contribute and make a real difference and then a bigger difference to more people as I refined my leadership through experience.

I had the privilege of working for two mayors in Houston, Texas the fourth largest city in the United States, a city growing, prospering and focusing on innovation and entrepreneurship as never before. As the head of the City of Houston's Human Resources, myself and my large HR staff of 250 people were responsible for about 22,000 of the city's employees (68,000) and their families and dependents. I worked on affordable housing, infrastructure and historical preservation and marshaled departmental budgets and contracts worth hundreds of millions of dollars in addition to pensions and retirement boards worth billions.

I helped design and teach MBA classes as a corporate fellow and helped prepare both graduates and undergraduates in schools of public affairs and public health. I was part of a special team collaborating on the future of public sector human resources. As someone who loves public speaking and giving presentations, I spoke across the country on topics of leadership, change, innovation and organizational transformation.

However, these leadership projects and experiences mean nothing if I was not M.A.D.— Making A Difference.

I'm writing this book to inspire, inform, motivate and educate and show you that if you are a supervisor, manager, executive or someone else who is just starting in a position of authority to get M.A.D. by boosting your leadership abilities and skills, regardless of your experience. I want to empower you with both new and advanced information that will help make you a stronger, better

INTRODUCTION

leader in any endeavor you are active in so that you can feel the great satisfaction of knowing that you've made a difference in your life and profession while making a difference for others.

We live in a time where leadership is more critical than ever to solve the escalating and accelerating problems, threats and challenges in just about every area of our lives and work. Exploding technological change, societal, political and environmental problems, economic uncertainty, political unrest, threats from rogue nations, and the list goes on. It all seems overwhelming to many of us. Leadership — good leadership and *more* good leadership — is desperately needed now. That's another reason I've chosen to do *M.A.D. Leadership* with a focus on special information that will advance your leadership, regardless of how skilled and experienced you are.

The topics and detailed information, strategies and techniques in my book are useful for actually every position level, whether supervisors, department managers and senior executives. And junior-to-senior leaders in any organization in government, the military, associations, non-profits and elsewhere will glean some "gold nuggets of wisdom" since my book is also the result, not only of my own experience and research but also from my discovering consummate leadership advice from so many other successful leaders I've known and worked with, wisdom and vital tips that I want to pass along to you. You'll find there are a multitude of "How-to's" in the book, but also a lot of "How-not-to's" as well — hundreds of prized tips, techniques, ideas, tactics and information-packed examples and "tools" you can use right away. At the end of each chapter, I summarize the key points with what I call "Omar's Bright Ideas."

With so many leadership books and articles out there already and hundreds (if not thousands) being published every year, what makes my book different? I decided to focus on both the substance and style of leadership. Substance, like one's character and abilities, are of paramount importance, but if a leader can also look the part, speak the part and act the part too, with a dash of panache, that element of style combined with the substance (character, knowledge, skills and behaviors) of leadership, can be an unbeatable combination that sets you apart and above others and provides for you a terrific competitive edge at work. In addition, and most importantly, the book is designed to actually be *enjoyable* to read. I hope and trust you will find it difficult to put down once started.

Without going into unnecessary detail, I'll summarize the content in my book for you. You'll read about various definitions, traits and styles of leadership in one of the beginning chapters. Then in a following one, you'll see how you, as a leader, can make a difference in your organization and also read about several fascinating people who did exceptional things with their lives. Terrific leaders are not just accomplished (perhaps even captivating) public speakers, but they also develop strong rapport and relationships with followers by being excellent, empathic listeners. My two chapters on speaking and listening cover lots of tips and ideas to help you strengthen those vital areas of communicating.

The two interesting chapters on charisma and presence will help enhance your overall image, credibility, gravitas, and your "connectedness" to others as a leader and give you ways to add dynamism, appeal and poise to your personality and stature. Encouragement and recognizing good work by management is a most important activity and behavior, yet studies show those in authority neglect to do it frequently, properly and sincerely. In that chapter, you'll get a multitude of ways to leverage encouragement for better employee engagement, morale and performance.

Experts say that about 80 percent of the success of a company that wants to accomplish more innovation and change is brought about by the organization's culture. You will appreciate the very useful, extraordinary detail about culture in that chapter that will help you shape your organization's culture. Then, there's my chapter about creativity and innovation that presents you with a powerful overview of these vital topics and includes insightful questions to assess how creative and innovative your organization is likely to be and how you can affect the culture.

The higher up you go on your leadership ladder, the more important it is to craft an enticing, beckoning vision for your company or group. My chapter on vision gives you bountiful ideas, tips and strategies to vividly "paint" a vision that excites and motivates your people. Militaries spent great deals of money, effort, and time to train all levels of their staff to be excellent leaders, whether in a tactical or strategic mode. In this extensive chapter, I share with you some invaluable learnings from several military greats that you can apply for an extraordinary effect in your career.

Please keep in mind that I've included quotations from people even from antiquity who use the male gender terms in them. Obviously, these quotations refer to females as well and that is my intention.

M.A.D. Leadership will help you recognize that before you are a leader, it's all about developing yourself. However, once you become a leader, it's all about developing your people and making as many leaders out of them as you can. There is an African Proverb that I use as the subtitle of my book and try to live by, "Show the people light and they will find their way." This book is dedicated to helping you be the light and show it. May you shine ever so brightly!

Chapter 1

Leadership
It's the Art and Skill of Making A Difference

"Success is not a function of the size of your title, but the richness of your contribution."
– Robin S. Sharma

I've been studying leadership for a long time and continuously working at being a better, stronger leader. I know the wonderful impact that masterful leadership will make in any organization, government, military, community, house of worship and elsewhere. The businessman and former president of the University of North Carolina system Erskine Bowles echoed my feelings and experiences when he said, "Leadership is the key to 99 percent of all successful efforts." In this chapter, I'll cover varied and interesting insights about leaders and leadership.

My two primary styles of leadership that I practice and sharpen are "Servant Leadership" and "Transformational Leadership," with my focus on encouraging and supporting creativity and innovation because these two styles enable my employees to best deal with the ferocious, accelerating change that we see throughout our world today. These two styles of leadership are at the heart of true, lasting success for all those involved — my managers, employees, teams, customers, partners and other stakeholders. After all, leadership is founded in relationships and developing, supporting and inspiring people, while leading and guiding with humility and humanity, will get you outstanding results.

I strive to create a growth and prosperity mindset for my teams and bring energy and optimism that are contagious. As leaders, we must set a pace that is brisk, but not hurried or frenetic. Otherwise, it results in burnout of people.

Throughout my book, I advocate rejecting the entrenched status quo that breeds mediocrity the longer it lasts and, instead, motivate my employees and teams to look for new ways to innovate and provide unmatched customer service. An integral part of my leadership agenda is helping to boost their performance on the job, resulting in their having a deep sense of pride, satisfaction and accomplishment, and, obviously contributing to my organization's success.

Robert Thomas, who worked with me prior to leading ADP's North American organizations, called me a business optimizer and people maximizer.

The best managers and leaders understand people and their motives, hopes, fears, drives and aspirations. Down deep, everyone wants to feel significant — that what they do and who they are has meaning, worth, fulfillment and dignity. They want to feel respected, appreciated and loved. Most want to be part of something noble, purposeful and bigger than themselves. Good leaders know how to psychologically tap into that human reservoir of feelings and emotions to best use and leverage their ideas, talents, desires, skills and ambitions for the good of all.

Donna Mitchell is one of the smartest benefits analysts you will meet. She needed an opportunity to shine. Her leadership had placed her in a box and was only using a small portion of her potential. When I met Donna, I immediately recognized her talent. As I had little experience in designing benefits programs, I knew that finding talent I could count on would be important. By empowering Donna and others during my time at the City of Houston we, Made A Difference in the lives of many city employees and their dependents.

Committed, real leaders are always leading whether in their business, associations, social circles, communities, political events, charitable organizations. It's "in their blood and DNA" to lead. I feel an obligation to lead like that in as many ways and places as I can. Good leaders embody the mindsets and actions to take charge and make a difference. Leadership by example is the only kind of genuine leadership that motivates and encourages others and builds vital trust with them. My teams will tell you I focus on behavior and character, not just competency. Whatever you preach, you must practice and be the change you want to see. General Charles C. Krulak, a retired U.S. Marine Corps officer who served as the Commandant of the Marine Corps from 1995 to 1999 stated, *"You cannot lead by memo, you cannot lead by shouting, you cannot lead by delegation of your responsibility — you must lead by example."*

Yet, I never cease to be amazed and shocked at the numbers of people who not only do not lead by example but who should not be in their positions. Those ineffective leaders over time pass bad attitudes and habits onto their direct reports, which can affect the quality of building a leadership pipeline besides damaging the organization's performance. Good leaders are those who consistently get excellent results while building capable, creative and committed individuals, teams and organizations. Sure, they make mistakes and wrong decisions and have setbacks. Who doesn't? But, overall and over time, their positive impact is evident to all.

Developing leaders is the top priority for a majority of various organizations, according to a recent survey of over 28,000 business leaders done by The Conference Board. Investments in leadership development through in-house training, books, micro-videos, podcasts, mentors, seminars, use of outside consultants and coaches and attendance at top universities doing executive education reflect that priority. According to recent data from the Chief Learning Officer (CLO) Business Intelligence Board, 94 percent of learning organizations either plan to increase or maintain their investment level for leadership development. Their top three leadership development goals are 1. Growing a succession pipeline (29%); 2. Retaining high-potential employees (19%); and 3. Fostering innovation and creative thinking (18%).

M.A.D.* LEADERSHIP

According to a report by Deloitte, corporations and organizations around the world place leadership development costs as high as a staggering $46 billion annually. A recent survey tells us there are over 15,000 leadership books in print with thousands of related articles being published every year. However, it seems to many that such a steep investment in upgrading the leadership abilities of people has minimal positive impact since many leaders and managers still

- don't get results or get them the wrong way;

- are poor communicators;

- fail to meet commitments and promises;

- take undeserved credit;

- are mediocre planners, strategists and implementors;

- micromanage to a fault;

- are self-serving, self-aggrandizing;

- deflect blame onto others;

- are risk-averse, playing it too safe;

- show favorites;

- deal in way too much internal politics;

- are lacking in vision and strategic thinking; and

- shirk accountability and responsibility.

1. LEADERSHIP

A Gallop poll in 2016 found that a scant 18 percent of managers show a high level of competency for managing others. So, a shocking 82 percent — little more than 8 out of 10 — of managers are doing a rather poor job of managing and supporting their employees. Gallop estimates this lack of leadership and management skills costs U.S. corporations up to $550 billion annually!

A study by the Corporate Leadership Council found that the billions of dollars spent on leadership training and development only improved productivity by 2 percent! So with all the vast amounts of money being spent on this training, why aren't we getting the results and returns on investment we want and expect? Just a few reasons are:

1. Some people just find it difficult-to-impossible to change their habits, even with serious efforts and good intentions. They revert to prior behaviors. In essence, with many of them, it's a fact that "you can't train a cat to be a dog."

2. The wrong people are promoted. Just because they have performed well as individual contributors, doesn't mean they will make successful managers. Also, the very traits of ambition, competitiveness, perfectionism and raw drive, unless tempered by "softening behaviors," are often the ones that hurt employees eventually.

3. Even though many are motivated to change and they "make a valiant effort," their organizational culture gradually saps their drive and enthusiasm to make a difference and their peers may be jealous and intimidated by their potential and try to sabotage them.

4. Power gets to them. Often, when managers and executives are on the fast track of increasing success and positional power in their organizations, they can become arrogant and tone-deaf to the ideas and needs of their employees with some turning into bullies. When many leaders start to feel powerful and more important, their benevolent qualities such as empathy and caring erode.

5. They have distorted views of themselves — inflated sense of self — along with their perceived proficiencies and behaviors. McKinsey & Company studied over 52,000 managers and employees in 2016 and found that leaders rated themselves as better and more competent than their employees rated them. This inaccurate self-perception can have a negative effect on relationships and employee engagement and performance. The helpful remedy is to have them get a 360-degree assessment that might prove surprising to them and help them convert their inflated perception into reality. For example, they often believe that they are better listeners, make good decisions and are open-minded, supportive and receptive to innovative approaches than their employees feel about them.

Those who evolve into better leaders learn by their mistakes, make a serious commitment to improve and embed their new knowledge, practices and skills on a daily basis. They are on guard to prevent getting puffed up and arrogant, especially after major achievements and work on staying relatively humble and approachable. They chase a higher purpose, not just a higher position. My friend Rick Winters once told me that the road to success is filled with many tempting parking spaces, but those who succeed keep driving forward.

Different Definitions and Observations of Leadership and Leaders

It's been estimated there are well over 500 definitions of leadership. Just about everyone has their own sense of what it is. Perhaps the only common denominator of what a leader is that he or she has followers. But each insight from a different definition perspective adds more substance to a topic that many find slippery to wrap their hands around. We can quickly spot leaders when we see and experience them, even within minutes from a first impression standpoint. But, ask people why they think that person is a leader and they often have difficulty explaining it in meaningful detail

When the term "leader" is brought up, a certain archetype typically comes to mind. In movies or TV, for example, straight from central casting, we see the polished, poised, articulate, well-dressed and groomed professional go-getter man or woman who effortlessly works 80 hours each week, never tiring, never sweating through the tough times and certainly never entertaining doubt or uncertainty. Always in control and wise to a fault, their spirit is indestructible. But, in real life, there are multitudes of very successful leaders who don't even come close to that iconic image, being good and decent "plow horses" instead of "show horses," who in their humility, stoical resolve and competence will accomplish whatever it ethically takes to make their organization great.

Pastor William Alexander Lawson is not your typical show horse leader, but his accomplishments over the past 57 years have been nothing short of amazing. When you first meet him, you will be surprised by how humble he is, but his listening and communicating set him above and apart from most. In 1962, he started a church in his living room with 13 others and over the course of the next 47 years, his MAD leadership would influence many major social and political events across the country. One of the best days of my life was spent accompanying him on a trip where he shared many personal insights on life and leadership.

Some leaders are calm, dispassionate and reserved, while others are dynamos of high-energy and charisma. Some are physically attractive and packaged well and have that special "look" of a leader, others not so much. I've known accomplished leaders who, themselves, were not the least bit imaginative or innovative and some others who could shoot out spectacular ideas like an oral machine gun and, yet, still be open-minded to the ideas of others. Many leaders are patient listeners contrasted against those who become annoyed and irritable if the speaker didn't get to the bottom line pronto.

It's certainly tough to try to pigeonhole people with a "one size fits all" composite of the ideal leader because there are so many different types, styles, personalities and appearances of leaders who succeeded in their field. What follows is a well-rounded mix of definitions and insights about leadership and leaders from academics, authors, consultants and others who have studied influential leaders, done academic research or have led people themselves.

After I searched for many definitions, I found that there were some common threads and themes that come out in many of these definitions – leaders influence and inspire their followers, they create visions, and that leadership is a process. As you read the following, think of how your definition of leadership compares to these:

- ✓ "Leadership is all about people…and getting the most out of people. It is about conveying a sense of purpose in a selfless manner and creating conditions of trust while displaying moral and physical courage." – Colin Powell

- ✓ "Successful leadership is leading with the heart, not just the head. They possess qualities like empathy, compassion and courage." – Bill George

- ✓ "Leadership revolves around vision, ideas, direction and has more to do with inspiring people as to direction and goals than with day-to-day implementation." – John Sculley

- ✓ "Leadership is a process whereby an individual influences a group of individuals to achieve a common goal." – Peter Northouse

- ✓ "A real leader uses every issue, no matter how serious and sensitive, to ensure that at the end of the debate we should emerge stronger and more united than ever before." – Nelson Mandela

- ✓ "The job of a leader is to speak to the possibility." – Benjamin Zander

- ✓ "Leadership is about articulating visions, embodying values, and creating the environment within which things can be accomplished." – Richards and Engle

- ✓ U.S. Air Force on leadership: "Leadership is the art of influencing and directing people in such a way that will win their obedience, confidence, respect and loyal cooperation in achieving common objectives."

✓ U.S. Army on leadership: "An Army leader is anyone who by virtue of assumed role or assigned responsibility inspires and influences people to accomplish organizational goals. Army leaders motivate people both inside and outside the chain of command to pursue actions, focus thinking and shape decisions for the greater good of the organization."

✓ U.S. Navy's definition: "Leadership is the art, science, or gift by which a person is enabled and privileged to direct the thoughts, plans, and actions of others in such a manner as to obtain and command their obedience, their confidence, their respect, and their loyal cooperation."

✓ U.S. Marines historical view of leadership: "General Lejeune stated that leadership is *the sum of those qualities of intellect, human understanding and moral character that enable a person to inspire and to control a group of people successfully.*'"

✓ "I'm looking for a lot of men who have the infinite capacity to not know what can't be done." – Henry Ford

✓ "Leadership is a process of influencing others to understand and agree about what needs to be done and how to do it, and the process of facilitating individual and collective efforts to accomplish shared objectives." – Gary A. Yukl

✓ "A leader takes people where they want to go. A *great* leader takes people where they don't necessarily want to go, but out to be." – Rosalynn Carter

✓ "One measure of leadership is the caliber of people who choose to follow you." – Dennis Peer

✓ "The very essence of leadership is that you have a vision. It's got to be a vision you articulate clearly and forcefully on every occasion. You cannot blow an uncertain trumpet." – Theodore Hesburgh

✓ "Leadership is unlocking people's potential to become better." – Bill Bradley

Scott Adams, the creator of the Dilbert comic strip and author of several works of satire, gives this definition an amusing reality check, "A leader has to be somebody who's getting people to do things which don't seem to make sense to them or are not in their best interest — like convincing people that they should work 14 hours so that someone else can make more money."

Finally, here's my definition of leadership is "Leadership is having courage and motivating, inspiring, and maximizing the potential of those whom you lead. It's putting others in a position to succeed by creating opportunities to help them exceed their own recognized potential."

Some Suggested Approaches to Becoming a Better Leader

How do you become a leader or how do you advance and enhance the leadership abilities you currently have? You must look the part, act the part and BE the leader. Leadership involves a complex set of behaviors, and my book will give you lots of insights, tips and techniques to build your "leadership muscle," regardless of your age, education, race, gender, social status or occupation. Becoming a leader, while it's more complicated, is like learning a sport, playing an instrument, learning how to fly a plane or becoming accomplished in any craft, profession or activity — you just methodically and continuously learn new things, practice, practice, practice, be patient (especially when things don't go as you planned or hoped), get lots of feedback and advice from others and just improve bit-by= bit.

My friend, Dr. Zenglo Chen, talks about paradoxical leadership. When you first become a leader, you're going to make mistakes. As you progress in your leadership journey and mature through stages, the magnitude of your mistakes should diminish.

Let me tell you about a mistake I made shortly after joining the City of Houston. Mayor Parker and a senior delegation had gone on a trade mission to China and left me in charge of putting a panel together to hire the next fire chief. During the communication, I selected a member that was a political opponent, and when she returned, the conversation was less than favorable for me. Needless to say, I learned to be a better listener and never made the same mistake.

If you haven't done it yet, it's very useful to take assessments to know more about yourself — how you make decisions, what is your emotional intelligence, how you interact with others, what your dominant personality and leadership behaviors and styles are and much more. Myers-Briggs (MBTI), Birkman Test, Goleman's EQ Test, the Enneagram Type Indicator are just a few. Some leadership assessment tools (useful for line employees too) are the DISC Assessment, Workplace Motivators Assessment, TriMetrixHD, USC's Leadership Style Self-Assessment, APT Metrics, and Leadership 360° are just a few. Another valuable assessment to see how you solve problems and innovate is the (Kirton Adaptation-Innovation Inventory (KAI).

Always put yourself into situations where you are asked or volunteer to lead a team, a project, or some other activity where you work with others toward a goal or some kind of win. Get a mentor or coach if you can. Carefully observe what experienced, competent managers, high-level executives and leaders do and identify what they do that really stands out and above others. Read my book carefully and read it several times, if need be. Also, read more books on different aspects of leadership. Each one can give you a valuable perspective or that one "golden nugget" of advice to use right away.

Read the Bible and learn how leaders from the Old and New Testament and how Jesus led multitudes of devoted followers. There's a treasure house of wisdom within it that can help you on the job. Study great leaders and business icons like Colin Powell, Steve Jobs, Teddy Roosevelt, Winston Churchill, Jeff Bezos, Abraham Lincoln, Martin Luther King, Jr., Elon Musk, Franklin D. Roosevelt, Nelson Mandela, Jack Welch and so many others who have changed their companies, militaries, cities, nations and even the world. Discover how a former actor Ronald Reagan and community organizer Barack Obama ascended to the highest office in the land through their leadership.

Read about or watch documentaries of great military leaders and commanders like Alexander the Great, Hannibal, Julius Caesar, Napoleon, Shaka Zulu, Geronimo, Ulysses S. Grant, William ("Billy") Mitchell, and the brilliant strategists and innovators of World War Two such as Douglas MacArthur, Chester Nimitz, Dwight D. Eisenhower, George S Patton and Georgi Zhukov. You can discover great insights on strategy, leadership and much more from them. There are excellent leadership books about U.S. Navy SEALs, Army Delta Force and Army Rangers and how these elite warriors exceptionally lead and what business can learn from them. Our military has some of the finest advanced leadership training and leaders in the world, and we can harvest a lot from them.

Look at free videos on YouTube on the topics of leadership, innovation, organizational change, emotional intelligence, building teams and a vast array of other leadership-related information. Watch motivational leaders speaking to groups to see how they influence and inspire them. Go to seminars and take advantage of every training opportunity your company offers. Remember that your experiences as a leader, sometimes with its downturns and occasional disappointing setbacks, should be seen as learning lessons for you to improve and avoid those typical mistakes that we all make, even after we've been at it for some time. While my book is specially designed and written to give you valuable "stuff" to make you a better leader, as with any activity, skill or talent, experience is the best exercise to build our "leadership muscle memory." Guess what? I'm still learning in pursuing leadership excellence, not perfection (which is unattainable).

Omar's 25 Initial Bright Ideas for You to Make A Difference

In each chapter of my book, I end it with what I call "Omar's Bright Ideas," which is a brief summary of the key points I discussed in that chapter. In the following, I want to share with you some initial overall thoughts about what I've learned about being a better leader that sets the stage for later chapters:

1. Leadership is personal, not positional. Regardless of your position on the organizational chart, you can be a leader who gets results with and through others.

2. The most important leadership characteristics are integrity, courage, humility, teamwork accountability and passion.

3. What gets recognized and rewarded, gets repeated and gets better. Good leaders will quickly acknowledge and show appreciation for those "doing the right things in the right ways."

4. While competencies are important in a leadership role, ethics, values and behaviors are paramount.

5. Due to the human spirit that we all are born with, we have a will to win. However, not everyone is born or disciplined with the will to *prepare* to win.

6. Human Resources is about people, process and procedures, but people should always come first. The biggest waste in organizations is not that of natural resources, but human resources. Benjamin Franklin said, "Most people die at twenty-five, but are not buried under seventy-five."

7. There is a necessary maturation process in becoming an effective leader. If you accelerate through the process too fast, you can miss important developmental steps.

8. As a Senior Vice President, my level of leadership calls for me to focus primarily on vision, change and innovation, not supervision or mundane details.

9. Relationship-based leadership requires an understanding of the world followers live in — their experiences, backgrounds, needs, wants, hopes, dreams, struggles, fears, pains and joys.

10. Activity does not equal accomplishment. Flapping your arms will not make you fly!

11. Before you become a leader, it's all about developing and preparing yourself for bigger roles and responsibilities. Once you become that leader, it's all about developing your staff and teams.

12. Absent accurate information, people will reach their own conclusion or answer. They will take just a piece of the puzzle and make a picture out of it. Using *Data Analytics*, the science of analyzing raw data to make informed decisions, plans and strategies from it, is a powerful tool for leaders to help everyone "fill in the puzzle." Realize, though, that leadership involves making decisions with less-than-complete information.

13. *Connect, Collaborate and Create* versus *Command and Control* leadership is changing organizational performance because of today's smart, diverse groups of people working creatively. Several of us can come up with a more powerful idea that I can alone. My job as a leader then becomes an encourager, supporter and facilitator of great ideas, not the dictator of the idea I originally came up with.

14. Two assets in life are time and money. The one we are running out of is time. Leaders succeed because of deliberate and intentional actions within a time constraint. The most powerful person in the world can't make more time, nor can the richest purchase one more second. How we best use time is up to us.

15. Comfortable, compliant and content can't be part of the conversation when talking about leading vital, needed change. You can share hard, candid truths without losing a sense of optimism. You must be committed, innovative, disruptive and transformative.

16. The people you associate with, the books you read, the videos you watch and everything else that flows into your mind and heart will affect the person you will become.

17. My 26 years at UPS (with 24 in management) taught me how to learn from "failures." It also taught me the immense value of being resilient — to bounce back and higher than before. Failure, however unwelcomed, is a necessary and useful part of growth. If you have not had to overcome obstacles, your ability to act under pressure is questioned.

18. It's not enough to be compliant with the right rules — you have to fully committed to the outcome to results to success to winning!

19. Today's employers who experience unprecedented levels of competition and frenetic change of all kinds seek to hire people with the ability to solve complex problems, work as a unified, creative team, possess emotional intelligence and be able to execute consistently.

20. A great leader is a "Business Optimizer" and "People Maximizer." Look for ways to improve organizational processes and make sure resources and structure are aligned properly. Remove as many

obstacles, red tape, needless complexity, bureaucracy and counterproductive politics as possible.

21. Three fundamental rules in a relationship are a) *Trust* is the basis of a husband/wife, employer/employee and pastor/parishioner, for example; b) *Communication.* We have two ears and one mouth, which means we should listen more than we talk; c) *Empathy.* You must be able to see and even feel things from the other person's perspective.

22. Success = Opportunity + Preparation. Regardless of how many opportunities might come your way, if you aren't prepared to take advantage of it, failure is the likely outcome. In addition, extreme preparation will not lead to success if you never receive an opportunity. To get in the game to score, prepare and be ready for opportunities every day.

23. Distill complex ideas, concepts, messages and possible solutions into a few simple sentences (including great visuals) so people can understand, appreciate and be interested in learning more about it.

24. Successful leaders are ultimately judged by action, action, action, results, results, results — all done with integrity.

25. "MAKE THE DASH COUNT!" We're on this earth a relatively little while. There is a tombstone right above a person when he or she is buried. On that tombstone, there is one's date of birth and your date of passing. Between those two dates, there is a dash mark. It indicates how you were M.A.D. — Making Difference — in your life and with others. "Why fit in when you were born to stand out," remarked Dr. Seuss. Good point!

Chapter 2

Are You M.A.D.

Making A Difference Through Your Leadership and Your Life?

"No individual has any right to come into the world and go out of
it without leaving behind him distinct and legitimate reasons for
having passed"
– George Washington Carver

I titled my book *M.A.D. (Make A Difference) Leadership. Give the People. Light and They Will Find Their Way* because I so admire and respect anyone, especially those good leaders who make a real difference in their lives and work. For many years I wanted to write a book that would encourage and help managers and leaders be the best they can in that regard. Now, you're reading it. Denzel Washington said it right, and it hit home with me, "Don't aspire to make a living, aspire to make a difference." Well-known Pastor Charles Stanley asked, "Do you want to impress people, or do you want to impact their lives — allowing God to work through you to transform them?"

On my personal emails, I always end them with "Blessed to be a blessing to others." I believe we are born and put on this earth to leave it a better place for as many people as we can. President John F. Kennedy noted, "One person can make a difference, and everyone should try." In this chapter, I will discuss how anyone, but especially leaders, can make a difference in their own lives and jobs, and most importantly, in the lives of many others.

In my motivational speeches and individual coaching sessions, I tell people to "Make Your Dash Count!" I often pause for several seconds as the person or group I'm talking with gives me a quizzical look. Then I tell them that we're living a relatively short period of time, and time seems to speed up, especially as we age. And when we pass away, if we have a tombstone, it has our name engraved on it with our year of birth and year of death. Between those two most important dates, there is a deciding dash mark, which tells how long we lived, but not what we've done with our lives.

I spend time talking about the basic, but important options all of us have in life — some having more than others — and the energy we spend during that "dash time." Up to this point, I ask, "What did we do with our lives? What did it count for?" It gets people thinking and wondering. Anyone and everyone can make that dash amount to something of significance with our own life, with our family, co-workers, people you worship with and everyone in whom we come in contact, even later in life. And, it's not necessarily about becoming a huge success in business, government, the military or elsewhere. Making the dash count is primarily about how we positively affected the lives of those who most needed it.

I sometimes drive the church van on Sunday. I have the pleasure of picking up members who live close by but don't necessarily have transportation to church. I picked up Ms. Dorothy Thomas from her residence. As she hopped in the front seat and gave me directions, she told me she was 96 years old. She told me that after service, she would not need a ride home as she would be leaving our service to teach Sunday School at another church. Ms. Thomas is a difference-maker who impacts the lives of others.

President Theodore Roosevelt was an exceptionally strong leader of integrity, character, courage and selflessness. He never felt that fame or riches were the best measures of success, "If a man lives a decent life and does his work fairly and squarely so that those dependent upon him and attached to him are better for his having lived, then he is a success." All of us can live a life of success that truly matters by making a personal and professional difference in hundreds or even thousands of small ways along our dash.

We can volunteer, donate money and articles to charitable causes, mentor young people, empathically listen to those hurting, encourage and support others in their difficult walk of life, be patient and respectful when someone annoys or criticizes you, teach, coach and share life lessons, motivate and inspire those longing for their dreams, visit and help the elderly or those who are sick or suffering like wounded warriors. The list of your making a difference is endless. The ancient Greek storyteller Aesop, who was famous for his fables noted, "No act of kindness no matter how small is ever wasted." As we'll see, leaders can have that extra leverage to make a bigger difference, simply because of their position, authority and stature with followers or employees.

Mother Teresa once said, "If you cannot feed a hundred people, feed one" and added, "In this life, we cannot always do great things. But we can do small things with great love." There's a simple, but I think profound story that you might have heard that echoes this idea of doing even a small act of goodness. One day, a man was walking along a beach littered with hundreds or more of starfish washed ashore by the high tide. As he walked near the water, he came upon a young boy picking up and gently throwing the starfish back into the ocean, one by one.

Puzzled and curious, the man looked at the boy and asked what he was doing. Without looking up from his mission, the boy matter-of-factly replied, "I'm saving these starfish, Sir. The sun is rising and the tide is going out. If I didn't throw them back, they'll die. I want them to live." The man smiled and said, "Young man, there are way too many starfish on this beach and only one of you. How can you possibly make a difference?" The boy picked up a starfish and gently tossed it into the water to save it. Turning to the man, he said, "I made a difference to that one." So too can we make a difference to "that one," whoever a person, animal or other living thing it may be.

Many people may not know that actor Denzel Washington is also a powerful and inspiring motivational speaker who tells his audiences, "So you never know who you touch. You never know how or when you'll have an impact, or how important your example can be to someone else. At the end of the day, it's not about what you have or even what you've accomplished. It's about what you've done with those accomplishments. It's about who you've lifted up, who you've made better. It's about what you've given back."

Look at the word "difference", and you'll see that it means a change in or effect on a situation or person. That's what Denzel was talking about. I believe God has put us on this earth to not only worship Him and live the life he has planned for us but also to make a difference — a change — that matters. Let's face it; it's not what you've done or where you were in the past — before in your life — but where you are now by starting out to make even more of an impact, and where you'll eventually end up by doing those worthy acts of kindness, goodness and generosity.

What a Difference He Made in So Many Ways

He was an amazing person of great ethical character, reputation and world-class achievements bestowed with great honors, celebrity and international fame. Yet, throughout his life, he was a noble, dignified and devoted Christian and humble person, even though he was a hero to countless people (both African Americans and whites). George Washington Carver (1860s-1943) was a top leader in his fields — an American agronomist, experimenter, researcher and agricultural chemist who helped revolutionize the agricultural economy of the South through product developments primarily from peanuts, soybeans and sweet potatoes.

Born into slavery, this African American became one of the most prominent inventors and scientists of his time as well as a respected educator at the Tuskegee Institute in spite of overwhelming and daunting adversity, racism and obstacles he faced. He craved an education so badly, he moved anywhere to get it, obtaining a Bachelor of Science degree in botany from Iowa State Agricultural School and later a Master of Agriculture. The search for knowledge was a driving force for Carver. In his earlier years, he moved from one Midwestern town to another, putting himself through schools and supported himself by varied occupations that included being a household worker, homesteader, hotel cook, laundryman and farm laborer.

2. ARE YOU M.A.D.

He was a leader in environmentalism before people actually realized what and how important it was. Agriculture in the Deep South was in decline because the single-crop long-term cultivation of cotton left the soil of numerous fields worthless because of depletion of vital nitrogen and erosion hurt areas that could no longer sustain any plants. Carver conducted experiments in soil management and crop production, and as a remedy, he urged Southern farmers to plant peanuts and soybeans to restore nitrogen in the fields while also providing badly needed sources of protein in the diet of many Southerners. His idea of crop rotation proved extremely valuable.

His inventions include over 300 various industrial and commercial products derived from peanuts, including Worcestershire sauce, milk, punches, plastics, paints, cosmetics, dyes, cooking and medicinal oils, soap, ink, wood stains and others. From sweet potatoes, he created 118 products such as postage stamp glue, flour, molasses, vinegar and synthetic rubber and even a form of gasoline!

He taught as a professor at Tuskegee Institute and was beloved by his students. As an educational innovator, he designed a mobile classroom to actually take education to farmers. While he focused on his students' academic development, he was also concerned with building and strengthening their characters. Carver composed eight cardinal virtues he encouraged his students to strive toward. This is great advice, especially with today's shrinking good values and disheartening behaviors:

1. Be clean both inside and out.

2. Neither look up to the rich nor down on the poor.

3. Lose, if need be, without squealing.

4. Win without bragging.

5. Always be considerate of women, children, and older people.

6. Be too brave to lie.

7. Be too generous to cheat.

8. Take your share of the world and let others take theirs.

Carver leveraged his celebrity and reputation to promote scientific causes throughout his life, even toward the remainder of it. He toured the country and wrote a syndicated newspaper column highlighting the critical nature of agricultural innovation and the breakthrough achievements at Tuskegee. He traveled the South to promote racial harmony and went to India to advise Mahatma Gandhi about agriculture and nutrition matters.

Throughout his most impressive life, he made many influential friends (like Henry Ford) and received numerous honors including being made a member of the British Royal Society of Arts in 1916 — a rare honor for an American. Shortly after Carver died on January 5, 1943 at Tuskegee Institute, President Franklin D. Roosevelt signed legislation for him to receive his own prestigious monument — the George Washington Carver Monument in Diamond, Missouri — an unprecedented honor previously granted only to presidents George Washington and Abraham Lincoln. Carver was also posthumously inducted into the National Inventors Hall of Fame.

Even great people have their critics and Carver responded to them with this sage comment, "When you do the common things in life in an uncommon way, you will command the attention of the world." His epitaph reads: "He could have added fortune to fame, but caring for neither, he found happiness and honor in being helpful to the world." What inspired him to do what he did was his faith in God and his love for humanity. He was truly the embodiment of a M.A.D. (Making A Difference) person throughout his exceptional life!

2. ARE YOU M.A.D.

A Woman of Absolutely Extraordinary Depth of Character

There are those transcendent people who amaze us with their incredible sacrifice, courage and daring risk-taking that give us hope that human nature is still good and decent in these trying times. This is a story that unmistakably shows that. At the beginning of World War II, the Nazis outlawed helping Jews in Poland, making not only the man or woman providing assistance punishable by death but also that person's entire family as well. Irena Stanisława Sendler, commonly known as Irena Sendler, was a Polish social worker and nurse active in the Polish underground in German-occupied Warsaw, the capital of Poland.

She knew the immense danger of saving these children from the Holocaust. Despite that, she risked everything to save close to 2,500 Jewish children. Sendler and other supporters smuggled children out of the Warsaw Ghetto and created false identity papers — over 3,000 "legitimate-looking" documents over four years. Sendler would enter the ghettos, sneaking in food, medicine, clothing and other needed items. In those now empty vehicles that drove away were hidden babies and small children. When no other methods of hiding them were available, children were creatively loaded into packages and suitcases. She gave the children to other brave and willing Polish families, orphanages and Catholic convents for nuns. Her goal was to keep the children safe until the war ended and then return them to their families, so she kept meticulous records of the children's whereabouts, along with their new and given names. These detailed lists she kept hidden in jars buried in the ground.

The Gestapo, the secret police of Nazi Germany, suspected Sendler of underground involvement and in October 1943, arrested her. Despite her imprisonment, brutal torture and being sentenced to death, she revealed nothing about the work she did and the names and locations of the children. She narrowly escaped the day of her execution because of German officials being bribed to obtain her release.

As she later told her story, she attributed the deep values that inspired her commitment to her work by her upbringing, "I was taught by my father that when someone is drowning, you don't ask if they can swim, you just jump in and help." She died in 2008 at 98. While still relatively unknown, she received numerous awards, including a nomination for the Novel Peace Prize, for her incredible dedication, courage and selflessness. To say she made a difference in her life and in those of the thousands of children is an understatement of monumental proportion.

"When Life Gave Him Lemons, He Built an Entire Lemonade Business"

How can you make a difference in anything when life deals you what seems like a totally losing hand of cards? Ask that of Nicholas James Vujicic. He was born in Melbourne, Australia in December 1982 with *tetra-amelia syndrome*, a very rare disorder (called *phocomelia*). He had no arms and visible legs. In his autobiography, he tells how his mother refused to see him or even hold him when the nurse presented him in front of her. But she and her husband eventually accepted his debilitating condition and saw it as "God's plan for their son." And, what a miraculous plan it turned out to be!

Vujicic has two (almost invisible) deformed feet, one of which he calls his "chicken drumstick" because of its shape. He learned to use his "foot" to operate a computer, electric wheelchair and his cell phone and do as much as he could by himself. As a young adult, he was bullied and attempted suicide at the age of 10, but in spite of that, he worked on constantly developing a positive attitude that helped him in his young adult years despite the heartache of his unbelievable condition. When he was seventeen, his mother showed him a newspaper article about a man dealing with a severe disability and an encounter with a janitor in his high school that year motivated him to learn about and start doing public speaking, including giving talks to his prayer group.

Over the years, he became a devoted Christian evangelist and a powerful motivational leader. This charismatic speaker has traveled to almost 60 countries and shared his fantastically inspiring story and emotionally-moving speech with confidence, humor and infectious hope to millions of people. Not one to limit his thinking, attitude and quest for a rich, full life, in 2008 in

McKinney, Texas (near Dallas) he met Kanae Miyahara and got married four years later. They now have four children and they live in Southern California. He graduated from Griffith University at 21 and wrote eight books. His first one, *Life Without Limits: Inspiration for a Ridiculously Good Life,* was published in 2010 and was translated into over 30 languages. Vujicic learned how to swim, surf and even skydive, all without arms and legs!

He's an amazing example of someone who conquered his condition physically, mentally and emotionally and developed a "winning hand in the cards of life." He was M.A.D. (Making A Difference) — a huge difference — through his live performances, videos, books and DVDs by inspiring perhaps hundreds of millions of people to see things in a radically new and better way, so they could overcome their own difficulties, challenges and heartbreaks they might be experiencing. See his website at http://www.nickvujicic.com and don't miss his videos on YouTube. …Be prepared to be humbled!

Make A Difference in Your Job. Strive for Diligence and Excellence

Martin Luther King Jr. believed and preached that no job or work is insignificant and that if it "uplifts humanity, it has dignity and importance and should be undertaken with painstaking excellence." Any job that somehow contributes to the prosperity, security, health, welfare, happiness or quality of life of people makes a difference, sometimes in ways we will never know as Denzel mentioned. You can often find "pearls of wisdom" right in some social media postings. I came across this one I liked, "The razor blade is sharp, but can't cut a tree. The axe is strong but can't cut the hair. Everyone is important according to his/her own unique purpose and contribution in life. Never look down on someone unless you are admiring their shoes."

Reverend King would repeatedly point out that no work is menial when he fervently said, "If a man is called to be a street sweeper, he should sweep streets even as a Michelangelo painted, or Beethoven composed music or Shakespeare wrote poetry. He should sweep streets so well that all the hosts of heaven and earth will pause to say, 'Here lived a great street sweeper who did his job well.'" That quotation hit home to me when I thought back on the time when I started working with UPS, and my job was helping to maintain the trucks by checking the oil and coolant levels, air pressure in the tires and other preventive maintenance tasks, to ensure the trucks were ready and reliable for deliveries the next day.

I did that job daily with pride, and in my 17 months of doing it, we never lost an engine. And even though the mechanics did not know my name and called me "dipstick," I took it as an affectionate compliment that I was a part of their team.

When you're young, you often fail to realize that a relatively simple, even a boring job after you do it day in and day out like that has consequences if not done with a dedicated attitude and positive work ethic. I realized that what if a UPS driver was delivering important medicine or a medical device and the truck broke down, perhaps the person receiving the package might be not just inconvenienced, but in pain without it, or worse yet complicate his or her health situation. Maybe a young lady was waiting to see if she had an acceptance from a college and was due to receive a package of important documents and information relating to it and the truck broke down and delayed her getting it. All jobs can make a difference, somehow, someway to somebody.

How Can You — as a Leader — Make More of a Positive Difference?

Genuine, effective leaders have followers or employees eager for their direction, guidance and leadership in bringing about important change or accelerating strategic innovation in their organizations. You have the influential power, authority and the ability to delegate tasks and activities to meet your goals, to institute needed change, to improve operations and to make as much and big a difference as you see it. Your power may not necessarily be in a management or formal leadership position, but through your charisma, credibility, competence, professionalism and inner strength, you are a natural leader who will rally others around goals, change and innovations.

2. ARE YOU M.A.D.

Many successful leaders don't set out to be a "leader." Instead, they are motivated and driven to make a difference — to solve a problem, to take advantage of an opportunity, to right a wrong, to significantly improve a condition or situation, to bring about a new breakthrough in business, science or technology or maybe to change the world — "make a dent in the universe" as Steve Jobs would say. Leadership is not just about the role or the responsibility, but, instead, about the intent, the goal, the results and the impact made.

In her second year of law school, my daughter Briana joined the *Innonence Project* at Louisiana State University. She teamed with others who worked to get people who were imprisoned as juveniles paroled. I remember speaking with her after they picked up the first person from Angola State Penitentiary. They had made a difference and she was excited about the future for the recently parolled individual.

Leaders, especially those "Innovative Leaders," are visionaries and game-changers and the "tip of the spear" in any organization pushing/pulling, motivating, inspiring and emboldening followers moving always toward something of value. In times of distress, major upheavals or threats, brave leaders with spines of steel, often become more of revolutionaries, risk-takers, mavericks, disruptors, fomenters, trailblazers and die-hard innovators to secure and protect prosperity, safety, peace, growth or stability where conventional and cautious strategies that worked in the past would otherwise now miserably fail.

Making a Difference Quantitatively and Qualitatively

Quantitative leadership refers to those areas that can and should be measured, monitored and modified (if need be) in their organizations. Leaders are responsible for the following:

1. *Optimizing Operations.* With managers, teams and outside resources, leaders must ensure that their operations — the functions, activities,

transactions, events and projects — are as effective, productive, efficient, and high-quality as possible. Errors, waste, mistakes and cost structures have to be minimized. Unnecessary and burdensome rules, policies, procedures, "red tape" and a bloated bureaucracy (that got that way over time) need to be eliminated or at least shrunk.

2. *Boosting Financials.* The economic health of a company is paramount to its surviving and thriving, so leaders must ensure that revenues, profits, returns on assets and investments, risk and liquidity ratios and other financial metrics are at the top of their game.

3. *Ensuring Growth and Expansion of Business.* Leaders are responsible for ensuring that their organization grows at a safe and smart rate, which also includes bringing about creative strategic alliances and purchases of other companies that will improve its overall value proposition to customers, employees and investors.

4. *Making Capital and Human Investments.* You build and strengthen the offerings of your organization by wise investments in buildings, advanced equipment, technology, research and development, process and automated systems and anything else that gives an improved industry competitive edge and helps toward realizing the future vision.

Qualitative leadership involves all those ideas, strategies and actions taken to improve, retain, motivate and inspire employees or followers and to maintain an ideal work environment that maximizes the ability and engagement of people to solve tough problems, seek attractive opportunities and continuously innovate products, services and operations throughout the organization. Exemplary leadership truly matters to peoples' commitment at work, their enthusiasm to work hard and take the initiative, the worthwhile meaning they derive from their efforts and their overall potential to perform far beyond the ordinary.

2. ARE YOU M.A.D.

Transcendent leaders bring out the best in individuals, teams and organizations by planning and implementing these qualitative factors:

1. *Bring An Exciting Vision Into Life.* A compelling glimpse into a bright future gives people hope and faith that will keep them enthusiastically working toward it. The right vision is a challenging and satisfying adventure for those filled with passion and purpose. Smart, creative leaders craft a vision with plans and strategies to give their followers a roadmap to follow and work toward. A stunning vision without essential change is an attractive mirage, but a vision fueled by well-executed change and innovation can bring about miracles. Few things will make a difference as a vision that is reached, only to then have a new one — an even bigger and better one — to strive for. The human spirit craves and thrives on that.

2. *Employee Hiring and Development.* Smart new hire onboarding, extensive employee training, coaching and mentoring and on-going performance measurement and assessment is vital to maintaining their peak performance throughout an organization. Providing skills training and education is an important benefit to both the employees and the organization as their abilities and morale are elevated.

3. *Role Model Integrity and Productive Behavior.* If you are the type of leader who others respect and admire, you can powerfully inspire them in the way you ethically, professionally and conduct yourself with character that engenders trust and loyalty. You can influence their beliefs, attitudes, and most importantly, their values. It's a bonus if your followers like you (as a person) as well. It's critical, though, to gain credibility and for them not just to commend, but to emulate your good qualities. "Walking the Talk" always has a psychological and emotional impact on followers. People look up to leaders and it's an opportunity for those in positions of power to diligently role model good habits and positive traits and actions. Showing the boldness and daring to "do the impossible" when ominous times and situations demand it is a

symbolic and good psychological "kick in the pants" stimulant to galvanize your followers for support.

4. *Strengthening the Culture.* You can't measure it directly, and with scant exceptions, you can't see it, but you can sense it and feel it under the surface at work, even though most employees don't give it a passing outward thought. Yet, your culture is at the heart and soul, playing a vital role in your organization's long-term success. It evolves for better or worse and your job as a leader is "like a good wine to make sure it improves with age." It's one of the paramount responsibilities in qualitative leadership. Younger employees especially want to work in a culture that provides freedom, flexibility, creativity and one where even fun, enjoyment and a sense of deep satisfaction flourishes at work.

5. *Empowering Employees.* When you give free rein, encouragement and support to people to collaborate to generate lots of good ideas, to solve problems, to amplify possibilities, to seek out and grab opportunities that others will miss, and for them to actively participate in planning (with other leaders) for the best ways to execute and implement change and innovation on the job, you are showing qualitative leadership and making a true difference through it. Leaders show people and let them feel that what they do is important to help them see that what they their part of work, along with others, is bigger than they are and that their contribution has meaning and purpose, and of course, makes a difference.

6. *Recognize, Appreciate, Reward and Celebrate.* Doing these things will make a huge difference in keeping employees, motivating them and energizing them to continue excellence and innovation in their work. As I've said throughout my book, you must quickly (if not immediately) recognize and acknowlege something an employee or team did well and then reward that person or group. Sometimes a simple, "Thank you for (mention the specific accomplishment or behavior)!" might be all that is needed. Praise in front of others is psychologically moving if the person likes that type of recognition.

Think of all the ways you can show your appreciation, pride and respect for your people. Don't forget to celebrate (in a small or big fashion) individual and team accomplishments and wins.

When called to lead, you are called to advance, to move forward with progress, to create worthwhile results and outcomes. In that regard, good, decent leaders are always those who make a difference by "leaving a mark, not a scar." Former sixth U.S. President John Quincy Adams put it this way, "If your actions inspire others to dream more, learn more, do more and become more, you are a leader." The accomplished, well-loved actor Morgan Freeman advised us, "If you want to see a miracle, be the miracle." Small miracles will then come when we make a difference in ourselves and in others. Go ahead, and be a miracle worker. That's the wonder of M.A.D. Leadership!

Omar's Bright Ideas

Summary for You to Make a Difference in Your Life by Your Leadership

1. As a leader, you rise by lifting others. That means often leading from your heart and also being a servant leader. Famous guitarist Carlos Santana put that in perspective, "There is no greater reward than working from the heart and making a difference in the world."

2. Good, effective leaders have people who support them and their mission. As such, as a leader, you now have more power, people and resources to do bigger and better things you couldn't prior to your assuming leadership in your area.

3. Think about all the minor-to-major ways you've made a difference for others and look to the future with optimism you can make even more of a difference in many new and wonderful ways.

4. What is your vision and goal(s) to make an upgraded change in your personal and professional life that will build your character and your reputation that will inspire others?

5. As a manager or leader in your group or organization, what would be the ultimate difference you can make in the next 2-3 years, given sufficient time, support and resources?

6. If you focus on what I call the "5 Ds" — Desire, Drive, Discipline, Determination and Dedication — and combine those with passion and a sense of mission (even destiny) in your life, you will not only be successful, but will also benefit many others. We can choose to be affected by the world, or we can decide and act to affect the world and live a life that matters.

7. Keep in your mind and heart what Ralph Waldo Emerson said, "The purpose of life is not to be happy. It is to be useful, to be honorable, to be compassionate, to have it make some difference that you have lived and lived well."

8. Being M.A.D. — Making A Difference — means doing the right things and being the "right stuff," even when times are tough and you face problems, adversity or misfortune. George Bernard Shaw waxed philosophic when he said, "Life isn't about finding yourself. Life is about creating yourself." And, I'll add to that "… and creating yourself in the best way for the best results!"

Chapter 3

Leadership Traits and Styles
What is the "Makeup" of M.A.D. Leaders?

*"If your actions inspire others to dream more, learn more, do more
and become more, you are a leader."*
– John Quincy Adams

Being a leader is one of the most difficult and challenging, yet one of the most rewarding roles you can take on. It can't be said enough that leaders really do come in all sizes, shapes, personalities, backgrounds, characteristics, behaviors, skill inventories and styles. Academics and researchers have been trying to discover the "secret sauce," common denominators, strengths and makeup of what makes a great leader. Professor Joanne Ciulla, who focuses on leadership ethics at Rutgers Business School, noted, "Leadership is not a person or a position. It is a complex moral relationship between people, based on trust, obligation, commitment, emotion, and a shared vision of the good." Leadership is more than a position and can be done by teams (as a whole), not just by an individual. In this chapter, I'll cover important aspects of various leadership traits and styles and also give insights on the difference between the roles and responsibilities of a "manager" versus a "leader."

On a social media site was this posting, "Being a leader doesn't require a title and having that title doesn't make you one." How true. So, when we use the term "leader," I mean that a person has the "right stuff" to get others to follow him or her willingly and that it is not just a formal named position or title of power or authority. Leaders don't command excellence; they build excellence. Former President Ronald Reagan might have identified the essence of leadership when he said, "The greatest leader is not necessarily the one who does the greatest things. He is the one that gets people to do the greatest things."

Manager Versus Leader: How Different Are They, Really?

Not so much now, but once, leadership was hailed as the ultimate skill compared to management. So, people prided themselves on being a "leader," not just a "manager." In numerous publications, seminars and videos, the collective opinion on a manager's role was viewed less favorably and that it was a relic of the past and nowhere near as positively affecting and valuable as being a leader. Go online and see how many posts support that belief and tout the huge perceived difference between the two.

Leaders think and act strategically and coordinate the major factors bringing about organizational success, while managers (such as middle managers), who typically have a smaller role, usually think and act tactically. In the military, for example, a general would be planning in a big, broad way, using all resources to plot the victory of a large battle, considering the "whole picture," while lower-level officers and sergeants would be thinking and performing tactically on how to maneuver their smaller units (e.g., squads, companies, battalions) within the greater plan. Yet, make no mistake about it that NCOs (Non-Commissioned Officers) — sergeants — are like middle managers, the ones who get things done and implemented and are the critical backbone of their organizations. And NCOs are typically very good leaders. Doing both the strategic and tactical in an effective, smart and creative way paves the way to victory, however you describe it.

Leaders create a shared vision and mission for the years ahead and are primarily dedicated and pay great attention to how to ensure a better future for their organizations. The best ones focus on never-ending, positive change and innovation to maximize their organization's productivity, efficiency, effectiveness and quality. They look for ways to reimagine, remake and reinvent their companies to keep them continuously ahead of competitors.

3. LEADERSHIP TRAITS AND STYLES

Leaders are the *architects* of an organizational culture and infrastructure that fires up employees for peak creative performance, while managers are the *builders and implementors* of that culture and organizational improvement plan. Accomplished leaders know how to attract, retain, motivate and reward superb talent. Consummate leaders build other strong leaders and work tirelessly on strengthening key values and loyalty in their organizations. The Navy SEALs pride themselves on saying they are a team of leaders versus just a team with a leader.

Managers are responsible for "running an apparatus" — making sure their operations run smoothly and efficiently with minimum disruptions, problems, waste and errors. They hire and fire staff, assign work, build teams, coach, monitor and measure performance, disseminate information, provide skills training and solve problems with their employees and teams. Managers plan, organize, coordinate and help structure overall operations. First and foremost, managers build, control and sustain the process, systems and infrastructure of operations, while leaders work on preparing for the future with a compelling vision and plan while motivating, inspiring, supporting and encouraging their people and followers to reach that destination.

Management is about overseeing a group of individuals to complete a shared set of goals and objectives. A manager defines the goals of a project, breaks it up into tasks, assigns out responsibilities, measures individual and group progress, and controls the scope and progress of the project to ensure success. While managers are the effective administrators, leaders are the primary visionary change masters and innovators who mold their organization into a force for the years ahead. As you might have heard before, "Managers do things right and leaders do the right things." Both strong and competent managers and leaders are needed for success.

I support that there are a lot of common skills and behaviors shared by both and that good managers also play a pivotal role in boosting innovation and the overall success of any organization. Remember that there are managers who are good leaders and leaders with management skills. But there are generally distinctions between the roles and responsibilities of both managers and leaders.

Below is a table you might think gives a stark contrast and separation between the general functions and responsibilities of managers (mostly those of "average" or undistinguished competency) and those of effective leaders. Remember that there are crossovers in roles and behaviors between managers and leaders and they are not always two distinct entities in those situations.

Managers	Leaders
• Maintain status quo	• Change and innovate
• Focus on the short-term view	• Concentrate on long-term
• Solve problems	• Seek opportunities
• Control or avoid risks	• Take calculated "courageous" risks
• React to change	• Be proactive by leading change
• Push and pull people to targets	• Lead them to the mission and vision
• Make incremental improvements	• Seek breakthroughs & quantum leaps
• Be conventional	• Take unconventional actions
• Take credit for results	• Credit their teams and individuals
• Strictly adhere to rules and policies	• Bend, stretch or break them
• Tell, instruct, and command	• Persuade, influence and empower
• Make tactical plans with details	• Craft encompassing strategic plans
• Seldom compliment or reward	• Praise and reward the smallest improvements
• Think concretely and solve issues	• Imagine in a big and abstract way
• Give feedback	• Ask for feedback, listen and act upon it
• Is a copy and imitates	• Is unique and originates

• Has an eye on the bottom line	• Focuses on company horizon and growth
• Exercises power over staff	• Develops and shares power with others
• Have employees	• Have eager followers
• Focus on employees' weaknesses	• Emphasize the good and strengths
• Seek ideas and alliances internally	• Look everywhere for ideas and connections
• Are about process and procedures	• Are about people and making them leaders
• Provide answers	• Ask questions and seek best answers
• Cooperative and compliant	• Disruptive, transformative, groundbreaking
• Look for ways to cut costs	• Seek investments for competitive advantage
• Exercise power *over* people	• Develop power *with* competent people

I can't emphasize enough how people in positions of authority impact their employees. For example, in a *TINYpulse 2014 Employee Engagement & Organizational Culture Report* with over 500 organizations and over 200,000 anonymous responses participating, findings show that only 21 percent of employees feel strongly valued at work and 49 percent of employees are not satisfied with their direct supervisor.

People seldom get to choose the manager they will work for, but they always choose the leader they want to follow and in which they commit their energy, creativity and passion. Peter Drucker, the late, great management guru noted that management and leadership in today's world, where employees are fortunately not seen as undifferentiated cogs in a wheel, but valued assets with skills, talents and creativity, should not be widely separated in their functions, but research and surveys tell us they still are in many cases.

Valuable Leadership Traits, Characteristics and Values

Do you remember a unique manager or leader you have most admired, respected and trusted — someone who was a "natural leader" — a person who seemed to have all the critical qualities, personality and ethical character to get impressive results from people? Like most of use, you probably described this person as having certain ideal, special "somethings" that made him or her stand out and above others — characteristics that made that leader unforgettable, credible, and so capable in ways that enabled that icon of natural, impressive leadership to get superb results.

Myron Gray, the former COO officer for UPS, was a leader with a major impact on me as a leader. His understanding of business and people made him stand above and apart from other leaders I worked for. He combined personal integrity with business acumen and charisma to motivate those in his organization. During a visit to our beta test site, a visit we had prepared for weeks, he clarified that we were not meeting the expectations and needed to increase our efforts or face replacement. His ability to inspire the vision and instill the accountability left a profound impact on me.

The personality trait model and theory of leadership has been validated and is based on the characteristics and qualities of many leaders — both successful and unsuccessful — and is used to predict leadership effectiveness and success. Personality traits of leaders refer to their unique behavioral, mental attributes and functioning and their overall disposition that shows how they think, feel and act.

The resulting lists of traits serves as a yardstick and are then compared to those of potential leaders to assess their likelihood of success or failure. But the list of possible traits tends to be very long — overestimated 100 different traits of successful leaders in various leadership positions have been identified and over 600 general "personality traits" that are considered positive, neutral and negative.

The trait theory can be used by people at all levels in many organizations. Managers and leaders can utilize the information from the theory to evaluate their position in the organization and to assess how their position can be made stronger and better. Reviewing traits and characteristics makes people in positions of authority aware of their strengths and weaknesses and they get an understanding of how they can develop their leadership qualities.

Academics and others who research leaders attempted to identify such leadership characteristic factors related to them, such as:

- *Physical:* overall appearance, grooming, dress, height and weight.

- *Demographic:* age, education, socioeconomic status, occupation, income level.

- *Personality:* confidence, warmth, assertiveness, charisma, presence, risk-taking.

- *Intellect:* brightness, decisiveness, understanding, judgment, knowledge, insight.

- *Task-oriented:* planner, priority-setter, initiative, drive, persistence, methodical.

- *Sociability:* rapport and relationship-building, cooperativeness, friendliness, empathic, sensitive, tactful and diplomatic.

To give you an example of traits, here is just a brief random list (out of over an estimated 600) positive and negative personality and behavior characteristics of people. Which ones would you say describe you and which ones would say that most enhance anyone's leadership abilities and overall effectiveness?

Examples of Positive Traits and Characteristics

• adaptable	• adventurous
• appreciative	• articulate
• benevolent	• big-thinking
• calm	• charismatic
• charming	• cheerful
• compassionate	• confident
• creative	• courageous
• daring	• determined
• disciplined	• discreet
• earnest	• eloquent
• energetic	• enthusiastic
• fair	• forgiving
• focused	• friendly
• generous	• genuine
• gracious	• humble
• idealistic	• impartial
• innovative	• insightful
• logical	• methodical
• meticulous	• objective
• optimistic	• organized
• passionate	• patient
• perceptive	• personable
• persuasive	• polished
• positive	• prudent
• realistic	• reliable
• resourceful	• responsive
• secure	• selfless
• sophisticated	• steadfast
• thorough	• well-rounded
• wise	• witty

Examples of Negative Traits and Characteristics

• abrasive	• abrupt
• aloof	• anxious
• amoral	• apathetic
• argumentative	• arrogant
• boorish	• calculating
• callous	• careless
• cold	• complaining
• conceited	• crass
• critical	• deceitful
• discouraging	• disorganized
• disrespectful	• domineering
• egocentric	• erratic
• fearful	• frivolous
• greedy	• haughty
• hostile	• impatient
• impulsive	• insecure
• insensitive	• intolerant
• irritable	• naïve
• narcissistic	• narrow-minded
• negative	• neglectful
• obsessive	• petty
• pompous	• predatory
• pretentious	• reactive
• resentful	• rigid
• scheming	• selfish
• small-thinking	• superficial
• tactless	• tense
• timid	• unappreciative
• uncaring	• unreliable
• vindictive	• weak

Successful leaders typically have interests, abilities, behaviors and values different from those of the less effective people in positions of power or authority. Some leaders are quieter, less emotional and more intellectual than those who are highly energized, passionate and outwardly assertive, yet they have other positive traits and qualities that attract certain types of followers. Some leaders are subdued and reserved, while others are flamboyant and flashy. From my experience, though, the best leaders — the ones who last the longest and accomplish the most —all have certain core capabilities and characteristics, and the exercise of the traits and behaviors need to be relevant to the group being led and the situation facing all involved.

Through much research conducted in the last three decades of the 20th century, a set of core traits of successful leaders have been identified. However, know that people do not become leaders because they possess certain traits alone. These traits are not solely responsible for identifying whether a person will be a strong, successful leader or not, but they are essentially seen as preconditions that endow people with leadership potential. So, based upon my experiences and research, I've found that the most effective leaders will typically possess these traits and characteristics (although I'm sure you can add others as well):

1. **Confidence**. These people are self-assured and they show it, even in the most subtle ways. They are convinced they can and should lead in ways that get things done right. These leaders display their conviction and faith to do the job. That quiet confidence shows that a person is completely at ease with themselves, so people are naturally drawn to them. When a leader has rock-solid confidence combined with genuine humility, that's an unbeatable combination to attract committed followers.

2. **Crafting A Vision**. Because leaders are architects of the future 5, 10 or more years ahead, they "see" what their organization will look and act like and how much better it will be. So, with teams of imaginative "dreamers" and

practical "realists," they analyze, plan and strategize (like brilliant chess players) detailed "moves" and directions to reach that beckoning, compelling vision.

3. **Results-oriented.** When all is said and done, results, not effort counts. These leaders are defined by the exceptional, superior results they deliver — on time, on target and on budget. They hire, develop, motivate and reward others to produce desired payoffs. You'll find that "Innovative leaders aim for the stars and reach the moon." Mediocre, average or typical results have no place in the hearts and minds of these remarkable leaders.

4. **Positive Ambition.** This important character trait is a predictor of positive life outcomes whether one is a leader or not. A team of organizational psychology researchers recently studied the causes and consequences of ambition they defined as "the persistent and generalized striving for success, attainment, and accomplishment." While there are those ambitious people who see their efforts rewarded by promotions, more prestige, power and financial compensation, those people "high in achievement motivation desires" — those who want to be M.A.D. (Making A Difference) people — value the achievement of doing well, both for themselves and others, whether they receive those material rewards or not.

5. **Integrity and Honesty.** Leaders develop deep trust with their followers by keeping commitments they make and showing reliability, dependability and predictability. When they say something, you can be assured it is accurate and the truth, with no exaggeration or the slightest bit of fabrication. Outstanding leaders know the deep value of having a solid, impeccable character and role modeling and living it — "walking the talk" — for followers or employees.

Character is built upon and can change in a positive way based upon the unique traits, beliefs, attitudes, values, qualities and inner strengths of a person that defines the moral and ethical fiber of that individual. A person's observable behavior and actions are an indication of his or her character. One of the most effective ways to influence others is to have and project a solid reputation built on character and results. Those leaders who possess the "high ground" of an impeccable, flawless level of personal and professional integrity will stand out and above others.

6. **Calm and Self-Controlled.** People respect these stable leaders because they are "cool under fire" and have an even-tempered, calm demeanor. They maintain impressive composure under stress and don't overreact or let their emotions run wild. This trait of being poised, patient, moderate and emotionally solid and rational-thinking under the most fierce and chaotic situations earn this type of leader great esteem and admiration. Test pilots for the U.S. Air Force flying new, highly-advanced prototype aircraft and astronauts were selected, among other critical characteristics, based upon their ability to calmly handle extreme stress during dangerous situations in test flights and in space. They were touted to "have the right stuff."

7. **Energy, Drive and Hard Work.** Have you ever met a leader who seemed tired and listless — devoid of energy? I doubt it. Leaders have ample reserves of stamina, vitality, energy and drive, always taking the initiative and having the vigor to accomplish big things. The best leaders are at the front — leading — not being holed up in a fancy, huge office. They are frequently visiting offices, factories and other buildings, discovering first-hand the problems, challenges and important issues workers want to express to a trusted leader who will act upon them.

8. **Effective Communicators Who Listen and Ask Questions.** Highly successful executives, military officers and others in authority talk less and listen more — to everyone. They ask smart, probing questions to dig deep into the root causes of problems and to search out potential opportunities. But when they speak, they have "an economy of words" that have substantial meaning. Most leaders learn and develop dynamic public speaking skills that serve them well in getting and motivating followers to their mission or cause.

9. **Smart and Knowledgeable.** Clarence Randall, a lawyer, Chairman of the Board of Inland Steel and a presidential advisor aptly said, *"The leader must know, must know that he knows, and must be able to make it abundantly clear to those around him that he knows."* This means someone who is extremely competent, well-informed and educated on critical topics related to their position, job, organization and industry. In includes good judgment, strong analytical and problem-solving abilities and the skill to see abstract concepts that might erupt into possibilities and opportunities. This creates the credibility that builds confidence and trust in his or her employees or followers.

10. **Courageous and Brave**. Superior leaders don't take counsel of their fears or criticism from others. They don't hesitate taking risks or "doing the right thing" despite overwhelming opposition to it. There's often a nobility to them in that regard. There's a saying, "A frightened captain makes a frightened crew." In his 70 battles (to which he never lost one), Alexander the Great (356 – 323 BC) always led from the front with almost superhuman fearlessness, and that generated great courage to his warriors behind him. Leaders with exceptional character have the faith and tough-mindedness to stay in the fight and win regardless of the odds and adversity.

11. **Tenacity, Persistence and Perseverance.** Leaders simply do not give up when times are tough, even brutally so. Stick-to-it-ness is a vital trait of the finest leaders. Comedian Steve Martin, perhaps jokingly said, "Thankfully, perseverance is a great substitute for talent." Nelson Mandela noted, "After climbing a great hill, one only finds that there are more hills to climb." Obviously, perseverance, determination and patience, along with talent, competency, creativity and other powerful traits and qualities, are unbeatable combinations to win and achieve remarkable results.

12. **Emotional Intelligence (EQ).** Successful leaders have empathy for others. They are aware and sensitive to the needs, wants, concerns, fears, hopes and dreams of their followers or employees and they address and strive to help others achieve what they desire. EQ is about understanding, controlling and

expressing one's own emotions and to also effectively deal with relationships in an empathic and appropriate way. High character leaders know just how to motivate, inspire, engage and galvanize people to their cause, not just through intellectual reasoning and justification, but by tapping into and firing up the emotions of others in a non-manipulative way.

13. **Imaginative and Innovative.** As I've said numerous times before in my book, excellent leaders are about positive change, continuous improvement and innovation (both incremental and radical breakthroughs). They are always looking for the best ideas, solutions, possibilities and opportunities to exploit to benefit their organizations, customers, employees and other stakeholders. "Good" is never good enough for them. They build organizational cultures focused on transforming every activity into increasingly better ones on a never-ending journey. Mary Oliver, a poet, said it so eloquently, "Keep some room in your heart for the unimaginable."

14. **Accountable and Responsible.** Would you be interested in working for a manager or following a leader who blames his or her mistakes, bad decisions, outright failures or setbacks on other people? Accountability means responsible behavior and ownership of the results from themselves and their employees. It's been said that great managers, for example, take the lion's share of the blame when things go wrong and give a great deal more of credit to their teams when a win is achieved. True leaders always say "We" instead of "I." The gold standard requires accountability of one's self and also of all those working for you. I often said of my boss Mayor Anise Parker that "she did not get enough credit when things worked well and too much blame when things went wrong."

15. **Enthusiastic, Passionate and Optimistic.** Leaders are "merchants of the positive." Their enthusiasm, energy and highly optimistic attitude and outlook radiates outward and then inward to others and gives those a sense of hope that all is well or will get better. These leaders know that communicating even slight negativism or defeatism, like an outbreak of a virus, will spread and

"infect" others quickly. Passion gives a special aura to leaders and is the internal fire that builds a heated desire that pushes them forward. Oprah Winfrey said, "Passion is energy. Feel the power that comes from focusing on what excites you." Innovative leaders are especially passionate about doing things others only dream about. Apple's founder Steve Jobs said, "You have to be burning with an idea, or a problem, or a wrong that you want to right. If you're not passionate enough from the start, you'll never stick it out."

You might be interested to know that the U.S. Army gives "23 Traits of Character" they list for their NCOs and officers. They are 1. Bearing; 2. Confidence; 3. Courage; 4. Integrity; 5. Decisiveness; 6. Justice; 7. Endurance; 8. Tact; 9. Initiative; 10. Coolness; 11. Maturity; 12. Improvement; 13. Will; 14. Assertiveness; 15. Candor; 16. Sense of humor; 17. Competence; 18. Commitment; 19. Creativity; 20. Self-discipline; 21. Humility; 22. Flexibility; and 23. Empathy/Compassion.

Finally, one research study was conducted with approximately 4,000 people asking them to identify both positive and negative qualities that would make them either follow or not follow a leader. The top three positive ones in priority order were honesty, confidence and knowledge of a leader and the top negative traits were arrogance, dishonesty and selfishness.

Leadership Styles That Show How They Get Things Done

Did you ever take a "personality assessment" using any of the four quadrant instruments such as DISC, Myers-Briggs, Four Temperaments or Merrill-Wilson? They are basically derived from Carl Jung's four personality types. These "tests" help you discover your individual traits and characteristics and how you generally behave under various situations and how you interact with other personality types or styles. Well, there are also *Leadership Styles* that basically do the same in how people in positions of power deal with situations, generally behave and handle people they manage or lead.

The leadership styles approach and concept emerged from the Ohio State University leadership studies than began back in 1945. I've found that in some cases academics identified over 20 styles, but I'll just briefly cover the most common and most important ones. Usually, organizations hire and promote managers and executives whose leadership styles fit nicely into their cultures. And those founders of a company, for example, might mold their organizational cultures around their leadership styles. There are both positive and negative consequences from each of these various leadership styles of those in positions of power. They have an important bearing on how effectively an organization reaches its objectives and deals with future problems, challenges, threats, competition and opportunities.

Think about what your leadership style is and how effective it has been in getting you the results you want. Marshall Goldsmith, one of the fathers of leadership coaching, wrote a book on this subject, *"What got you here will not get you there."* While it may not be easy to change, you can likely improve yourself — even reinvent yourself — over time with the right resources, coaching, practice and assistance from others, if you choose. Look over the following leadership style types and see perhaps what you're doing right and what you might be missing.

Louis R. Mobley, the director of the executive school of IBM in the 1950s and 1960s highlighted that leadership is primarily based on experience, practice (learning from it) and developing good habits, not just intellect. According to him, success comes 20 percent from knowledge and 80 percent from behavior. That's why I wrote my book for you to give you a wide and deep spread of knowledge that can account for more than his belief of 20 percent of learning that will reduce your natural inclination to make mistakes on the job and learn from them.

Different leadership styles are needed for different situations, and conditions and each leader needs to know when and how to leverage a particular approach. The best leaders are those who are highly flexible, adaptable and capable and skilled enough to naturally switch gears in ways that still hold the trust and respect of their followers. There are times to strongly command, other times to let go and delegate and empower, times to ramp up the change machine, times to let off the throttle so people can regroup and rethink, times to follow the rules and times to disrupt the burdensome bureaucracy and dismantle it.

Command and Control Leadership Style

Often called the autocratic or "take charge" leadership style, this classical approach is likened to the old-style military aspect of leadership and still prevalent at many senior executive levels in organizations. Leaders express degrees of dominance in this style with the severe cases where the leaders demand immediate compliance so the staff is expected to obey orders receiving no explanations. The leader in this style "runs a tight ship" by planning, organizing, controlling, directing the efforts of others with minimal or no input or engagement on the part of lower-level managers or employees. They make decisions without consulting their support staff or team members. These leaders or managers can, in extreme cases, be overbearing, reluctant to get ideas from others and prone to using punishment more than motivating rewards and psychological incentives. "Do what you're told and do your job" is their style in a phrase.

Tight controls are used to assure that people do their jobs as defined and required. Usually, all but the most minor decisions must be made or approved by this leader. Communication is essentially one-way downward in a formal, structured, and impersonal fashion. With this type of leader, the sole emphasis is on performance, safety, order and results and low emphasis on and caring for people (who are often considered expendable by those types of strict and dogmatic executives).

This leadership style, however, can be highly effective in crisis situations with a strong, capable personality, but is the least effective way to manage or lead competent and creative people (at all levels) with ideas, solutions and strategies that would greatly contribute to the success of the organization. It can have a hurtful effect on the work climate given today's knowledge worker and can negatively affect employee engagement and retention. People feel restricted and demotivated, and this style of leadership limits others' ability to develop their own leadership skills. This is the worst leadership style for creative, entrepreneurial and innovative employees who need the freedom to explore ideas, solutions and approaches to their work.

Servant Leadership Style

This is the style I strive to use most of the time, combined with innovative and transformational leadership styles. With servant leadership, you have responsibility for your

followers or employees because you know that your success and the success of your organization really depends upon the best performance of your employees. For example, what good is a military general who has poorly trained, low morale troops who are forced to take orders, some of which they know are ill-planned and will be badly executed and will not be fully engaged in the fight? No general can fight a war and win with just other officers. They need troops (just like you need civilian workers) at all levels who are best trained, best equipped and best energized with a will to win. So, those generals and other higher-level officers must make sure their people have everything they need to do the job. And, therefore, it means sometimes using a servant leadership style, not just a commanding style all the time.

For the last ten years, I have personally had a 30-minute conversation with everyone who has come to work on my team. This introductory conversation allows me to show my interest in the persons responsible for our collective success. I want to meet them and make sure that we are off to a fast, good start.

The best servant leaders place the interests and needs of their followers or employees ahead of their own self-interests and needs. They act authentically, share power and value the development and growth of their followers who will make their organizations effective and efficient. A servant leader helps his or her employees by providing the right types and amounts of priority resources, training and development and by giving lots of encouragement, motivation, recognition and rewards that contribute to not only their professional growth but personal growth and wellness as well.

Servant leaders are not weak or passive in the least. They create the vision, mission, goals and strategies of their organization, but they do it cooperatively with and through others. They praise, encourage, hold accountable and inspire employees or followers and stakeholders. These leaders are excellent at listening, being empathic, and showing a nurturing spirit to others in ways that create a trusting environment and one filled with meaningful and joyful work, whenever possible.

Servant leadership is a very moral position, putting the well-being of their followers right on top. Some famous leaders of this practice include Martin Luther King, Jr., Mother Teresa, Albert Schweitzer and Nelson Mandela. The Container Store's CEO Kip Tindell has said that he does not believe in solely focusing on maximizing returns to shareholders as a core value. He always puts employees first. Sir Richard Branson, servant leader and founder of the Virgin Group in the 1970s (which controls over 400 companies) and a serial entrepreneur and philanthropist says, "By putting the employee first, the customer effectively comes first by default, and in the end, the shareholder comes first by default as well."

Hands Off Leadership Style

Also known as the laissez-faire leadership style, it can be a misnomer because, in its extreme negative form, there is no real leadership involved, just a person with a title or position of questionable authority going through the motions while having little or no credibility from his or her followers or employees. A person like this provides no guidance, direction or leadership and, instead, gives staff as much freedom and choice as possible. All power and decision making are given away to the staff for them to determine operational aspects such as setting goals, planning, creating solutions, forming teams and just about anything else. In the extreme form of this style, the "leader" ignores conflicts, problems and mistakes hoping they will somehow disappear.

However, sometimes, managers must keep a low profile and let their employees alone with a limited laissez-faire type of leadership mode. For example, if the staff is highly skilled, experienced, creative, trustworthy, self-motivated and takes initiative and pride in their work, this leader can have limited hands-off in a project (or series of them) to give them the warranted freedom to operate in a highly productive, effective and efficient way. But this manager or leader should still make sure that he or she supports their meaningful plans, provides necessary resources, communicates and gives them advice and feedback as appropriate, reduces any conflict and recognizes and rewards their achievements. "Hands off" never means always hands off — that's abdicating required leadership.

Charismatic Leadership Style

These leaders or managers influence, persuade and move others through the force of their appealing personality. They are passionate, highly confident, energetic, driven, often very charming and very motivating. People are naturally and "magnetically" drawn to them, especially if they are dynamic, captivating public speakers and excellent listeners. A charismatic leadership style excites, inspires, commits and galvanizes people to their visions, missions and plans. Leaders such as Martin Luther King, Jr., Oprah Winfrey, Steve Jobs, Barack Obama, Richard Branson, Winston Churchill, Nelson Mandela and John F. Kennedy are examples of people with aspects of this style. If employees are energized and engaged by these impressive leaders, what happens when they leave?

This leadership style is about one's personality and often attractive appearance. So, while other leaders can learn to be more charismatic, it's that "X Factor" that only select people possess. Organizations can become addicted to charismatic leaders, and a percentage of these personalities already are or will become narcissistic and self-serving after excessive affection, compliments and accolades are repeatedly thrown at them. However, a focused, ethical and selfless use of this leadership style is valuable and can arouse and fire up employees to peak performance, more risk-taking and give them a sense of adventure and accomplishment.

Transformational Leadership Style

These valuable leaders see and build the future. This style focuses on positive continuous change, improvement and innovation in every aspect of their organization. Right now, wise leaders know that technology is in an unprecedented explosive stage with AI (Artificial Intelligence), robotics, quantum computing, 3D printing, materials science and other radical technology and science breakthroughs about to rewrite history and affect all organizations as never before. These leaders will strive to change faster than change (or at least faster and better than their competitors) in as many areas as they realistically can related to their business.

Transformational Leadership is my dominant style (mixed in with Servant Leadership style) when I worked at UPS and The City of Houston and now at Harris Health System. I work to make change happen in myself (as a person and professional), in others, in my teams and throughout not just my area of responsibility, but my whole organization as I am able to do it to whatever extent. Transformational leaders often have charisma that helps enlist the aid of many others. Richard Branson, Steve Jobs, Martin Luther King, Jr., Nelson Mandela, Alexander the Great, Andrew Carnegie, Walt Disney, Henry Ford, Bill Gates, Mikhail Gorbachev and Ronald Reagan, Mary Barra (Chairman and CEO of General Motors) , Hyman Rickover (got the U.S. Navy to go nuclear power) and Sam Walton are just some of those who created major changes or accelerated and transformed them in the areas of science, industry, engineering, economics, business and technology.

Transformational leaders focus on both incremental innovations and quantum leaps and that results-focused leadership ideally reaches every level in the organization. They develop enticing and compelling visions that invite follows into a future of exciting opportunities. These leaders are usually excellent communicators, have high emotional intelligence (with strong empathy) and are skilled in building alliances, coalitions and partners to advance their goals. They make their employees their allies and expect superior performance from those they lead. Transformative Leaders are skillfully adaptable in how they handle challenging situations, problems, conflicts and politics in their organizations.

People will follow someone who inspires them to do great things together that they cannot do alone. "Transformers" inject enthusiasm, energy and gobs of optimism to get things done, and this psychologically affects people in their beliefs and hopes. They don't command, coerce, cajole or otherwise strong-arm employees, but use powers of persuasion to get an eager commitment. Transformational leadership creates valuable change in followers or employees with the end goal of developing followers into other strong leaders who accelerate the movement toward the organizational vision.

One important variation of this style takes Transformation Leadership up several notches. It's Innovative Leadership. Besides transforming their organization's vision, mission and goals, culture, systems and processes, products and services, policies and procedures, these transcendent leaders are fixated on being supremely innovative, both by themselves and through others. Examples of such leaders are Elon Musk (of Space X and Tesla Motors), Walt Disney, Steve Jobs, Jeff Bezos, Mark Zuckerberg, Henry Ford and Alexander the Great. While most transformational leaders promote, support and focus on innovation, these leaders are both creative and innovative themselves, proposing and implementing far-out, bodacious ideas, solutions, strategies, and concepts. But, most importantly, they hire, train and otherwise empower other extremely creative and innovative people to add to or otherwise improve and then commercialize their exceptional ideas.

3. LEADERSHIP TRAITS AND STYLES

Transactional Leadership Style

This approach to leadership emphasizes getting things done when the status quo is the preferred norm of the culture and operations. Precise order and structure are required and valued over change and innovation. This leader or manager goes "by the book," always working within the prescribed procedures and policies outlined in the organization, usually a large, bureaucratic one with a clear, defined chain of command. This style is prevalent and applicable to industries and businesses with repeatable procedures and processes such as manufacturing and various services that have established an effective transaction series of steps. These managers or leaders keep followers or employees motivated in the short term by using rewards, incentives, sanctions, and punishments.

Transactional leaders are likely to be in the military (especially logistics), in large, established corporations, or to be in charge of international projects that require stringent rules and regulations to complete goals and objectives on time, on budget and on target. Transactional leadership style operates in that that managers give employees something they want in exchange for getting something they want. It assumes that employees require order, direction and monitoring to complete tasks correctly and on time. So, when a transactional leader allocates work to an individual or team, they are considered responsible for it, sometimes even where they do not have the needed resources or ability to bring about expected results.

Transactional style is a "telling" leadership one, where transformational is a "selling" and persuasive influencing style. While the transactional approach involves positive and negative reinforcement, transformational leadership emphasizes support, engagement, motivation and inspiration. Transactional leaders are typically reactive because they often use "management by exception" — that if something is operating accordingly, then it needs no ongoing monitoring or other attention. So, when something unexpected occurs, the reaction happens. Transformational leaders are proactive with contingency options and plans. Transactional leadership appeals to the self-interest of individuals, while the transformational style prioritizes team and group functioning and performance. Transactional and transformational leadership can be effectively combined, however, for ideal outcomes for both leaders and their employees.

Omar's Bright Ideas

Summary of Making A Difference Through Leadership Traits and Styles

1. While personality traits and characteristics can help to identify and promote strong leadership, they alone do not make a leader, but almost all successful leaders possess the core 15 traits I described.

2. Managers are mostly about process and systems, leaders about people. Managers are tasked with keeping operations running smoothly and efficiently, and leaders are responsible for innovating the future, including creating a vision for the whole organization and getting people to bring it to reality.

3. The best way to identify and improve your leadership is through real-world experiences in addition to learning from books, seminars, webinars and videos, but experience is paramount.

4. There are managers who are good leaders and leaders who are good managers.

5. Studies show that most employees leave or stay because of their direct supervisor or manager, so their impact greatly affects employee retention, engagement and overall performance.

6. There are numerous leadership styles that people in positions of authority have. The best leadership style is flexible and adaptable enough to easily transition among each of those styles as the situation demands it for best results.

7. How can you really tell whether you are an effective leader, and how can you get even better? The strengths you have and the areas you need to improve can be identified if you got a 360-degree performance review in addition to using other assessments around leadership and management skills. You might be surprised at the findings!

8. Read about other great leaders and also those who failed to see common threads that led to their achievements or downfalls.

9. Always focus on the positive difference you can and should make through your leadership. Remember that what seems like leadership is often based on position or artificial power, while real leadership operates from authentic and earned power.

M.A.D.* LEADERSHIP

Chapter 4

Encouraging & Motivating Your People to Peak Performance

Letting Them Know You Appreciate, Care and Support Them

"The finest gift you can give anyone is encouragement. Yet, almost no one gets the encouragement they need to grow to their full potential. If everyone received the encouragement they need to grow, the genius in most everyone would blossom and the world would produce abundance beyond the wildest dreams. We would have more than one Einstein, Edison, Schweitzer, Mother Theresa, Dr. Salk and other great minds in a century."
– Poet Sidney Madwed

Leadership is about getting results through others. Leaders are tasked with creating a bright future for their followers, employees, organizations or city, area or country. Leaders, unlike "administrators," are not passive caretakers, squatters or keepers of the status quo. They are pioneers, opening new vistas and opportunities. They are trailblazers and movers and shakers. They must depend upon others, though, to fulfill their vision, goals and plans. Keeping followers motivated, engaged and inspired is vital to getting peak performance from them. That's why encouragement is one of the most important behaviors and skills a leader can develop because encouragement boosts performance, productivity and innovation. It strengthens morale and motivation and deepens a person's resolve and commitment to action and success. In this chapter, you'll discover approaches and behaviors to "boost" people so they can better be able to sustain peak levels of performance, successfully get through tough and challenging times and maintain a high quality of life at work.

Research shows that encouragement actually improves the physical, psychological and emotional well-being of people, especially when times are tough. One of the most insightful and visionary business leaders of the early 20th century was Charles Schwab, American steel magnate who founded Bethlehem Steel. He said, "I consider my ability to arouse enthusiasm among men the greatest asset I possess. The way to develop the best that is in a man is by appreciation and encouragement."

Effective leadership is also about exhibiting the right type of strength that encourages and motivates others. African-American leader and Tuskegee Institute founder Booker T. Washington, a man of utmost character and integrity, noted, "There are two ways of exerting one's strength: one is pushing down, the other is pulling up." Great leaders and managers lift their employees and followers up. And when they do that, they lift themselves up as well. Famous motivational speaker Zig Ziglar said, "When you encourage others, you in the process are encouraged because you're making a commitment and difference in that person's life.

Encouragement is the act of giving a person, teams or larger groups support, confidence and hope. Effectively using encouragement by praise, recognition and showing appreciation can be great assets —invaluable tools — in creating an exceptional environment and climate where positive relationships and peak performance will regularly flourish. According to a *Kepner-Tragoe* study, only about 40 percent of North American workers say they receive *any* recognition for a job well done, and that same 40 percent figure reports that they never get recognized for outstanding individual work performance.

During one stretch of my leadership at UPS, we were struggling with employee injuries. Almost daily someone in our operation was getting injured, so we posted our information each day. We told everyone that if we went one week without an injury, we would have a celebration. At the same time, we

4. ENCOURAGING & MOTIVATING YOUR PEOPLE TO PEAK PERFORMANCE

increased our auditing and education of proper safety behaviors. We celebrated at the end of the week and went on for several months with no injuries.

In the study, only 50 percent of the managers say they recognize high performance at work. These managers are knowingly negligent or just assume that providing outstanding, "beyond-the-call-of-duty" accomplishments are simply part of the job — sorry, no encouragement, praise or compliments needed. According to a *Workforce Mood Tracker* survey, 69 percent of employees would work harder if they were better recognized, and 78 percent said being recognized motivates them on the job.

How we connect with others as a leader has unimaginable significance in achieving our long-term goals and results while benefitting those we lead or work with. Words of encouragement are like energy pills that give us the strength and the will that we need to reach our objectives. With encouragement, we can work harder and longer to finish a tough task.

We all need encouragement. Sometimes we even need it desperately. If you've ever been on the sidelines of a runner's or biker's marathon, you, along with others, enthusiastically cheered them to press on despite fatigue, exhaustion or pain by exhorting them with shouts of "Keep going!" or "You can do it" or "Don't give up!" Runners appreciate yelling, clapping, or whistling as ways to urge them to the finish line. Passionate and encouraging pep talks from sports coaches inspire the players and give them hope and spur them to victory, especially during brutally tough competitions. Military leaders meet with troops face-to-face to show they care and to give them support and encouragement before battles or grueling non-conflict assignments.

For seven years, I have participated in the MS 150, a two-day bike ride from Houston, TX to the state capital Austin, TX. Day one, depending on the route, is 84 miles or more. The ride takes place in April and the weather in Texas during this time of year can be unpredictable. However, there is a consistent turnout in the city of Bellview, TX during the first day. As a tired rider, you can count on the residents to be out playing music, holding encouraging signs and generally encouraging us to keep pedaling. I appreciate them!

Do you need encouragement to perform at your best? You might say, "No, I'm a responsible, self-motivated and driven professional to do my best in spite of no feedback or support from others." I remember reading and taking notes years ago from a book that, unfortunately, I can't recall the title or author, but he said that his team asked people that type of question about requiring encouragement to work better. The author noted that only 60 percent said they needed encouragement to do their best while the other 40 percent said they didn't need it at all—they would do their best without it. Many of these people surveyed thought that by admitting they needed encouragement, it would imply they could not perform well unless someone was there to cheer them on. The author then cleverly reframed the question, "When you receive encouragement, does it help you perform at a higher level?" He noted that this time about 98 percent said yes!

Encouragement Has Different Faces with Numerous Benefits

The word itself has the prefix "en" which means "put into" or "bring to a certain state." So, when you view the whole term, en-courage, it means "bringing into a state of courage." The word "courage" can have important offshoots, a few being bravery, audacity, fearlessness, daring, valor, guts and spunk. Therefore, when we encourage people, we are attempting to help strengthen their backbone, confidence and resolve. David Jeremiah, Senior Pastor of Shadow Mountain Community Church in San Diego in his book, *The Joy of Encouragement. Unlock the Power of Building Others Up* writes:

"In the New Testament, the word most often translated as 'encouragement' is *parakalein*. This term comes from the Greek words: *para*, meaning 'alongside of,' and *kaleo*, meaning 'to call.' When people come alongside us during difficult times to give us renewed courage, a renewed spirit, renewed hope — that's encouragement."

4. ENCOURAGING & MOTIVATING YOUR PEOPLE TO PEAK PERFORMANCE

Pastor David Jeremiah noted that in the New Testament, the theme of encouragement is everywhere, especially in Apostle Paul's writings. Encouragement comes from the heart. It's heart-to-heart, not brain-to-heart. To better appreciate the emotional and psychological effects of encouraging people, here are synonyms for the term "encouragement." Look at all the different and wonderful aspects of words like it.

- applaud
- boost
- brighten
- buoy
- cheer
- comfort
- console
- embolden
- energize
- enliven
- fortify
- galvanize
- gladden
- inspire
- prop up
- rally
- reassure
- refresh
- revitalize
- spur

Encouragement builds self-esteem, fosters cooperation, celebrates special skills and talents and gives people hope. It helps to sustain them during those very tough or brutally disappointing or struggling times. It stiffens their spines, lifts their spirits and warms their hearts to carry on and makes a positive difference in their lives and in their work. Encouragement and praise empower people to learn new behaviors and skills and to improve the ones they already have. It's especially important for leaders and managers to encourage their followers and employees during complex, large-scale, demanding (often exhausting) innovation projects or painful organizational change events that involve fear, resistance, setbacks, obstacles and tough decisions affecting all those people involved.

Words and actions can lift up or tear down. At a meeting when someone proposes a creative idea, a simple thing like a frown, a smirk, an eye roll, a shrug, a sneer or a laugh from one or more people can kill a spark of insight and diminish further participation with the group. But when we build others up, they are more equipped and secure in ignoring the discouragement from naysayers and critics. Encouragement, even from just one person on the team or group (who is an "Angel's Advocate" instead of a typical "Devil's Advocate") who says, "Great idea. We should consider it!" will help that person who offered that imaginative idea to more eagerly go forward with the next step. When we are supported and appreciated instead of being put down, we can come back for more and keep fighting because we have a friend in our corner, not a negative someone(s) trying to pull the rug from under us.

Words of deep encouragement during a failure are healing and sustaining and worth more than an hour of praise after a success. The Apostle Paul, in the Bible (1 Thessalonians 5:11-15) exhorts Christians to encourage one another, particularly those who are disheartened. Never underestimate the power of encouragement! When someone encourages, motivates, praises and inspires you, your heart, the mind and soul are enriched.

4. ENCOURAGING & MOTIVATING YOUR PEOPLE TO PEAK PERFORMANCE

Language of Encouragement and Discouragement

These examples of statements contrast those that are uplifting, confidence-building and imply faith in the person's ability to succeed versus discouraging statements that convey doubt, possible disrespect and lack of faith in a person's skills or performance.

Encouragement Statements

- "I know you can do it."

- "You have the skills and talents to ace this project."

- "You're a dedicated, hard worker who will make it happen."

- "Your team and I have total trust and faith in your leadership."

- "Our future looks bright and exciting for our group and you will play a big role in it."

- "I've seen you in action. You're impressive and will succeed."

- "I'm looking forward to you and your team completely solving this engineering challenge!"

- "I need your advice and ideas. You're highly creative in these situations."

- "You will do your best. You always do."

- *Discouragement Statements*

- "Don't forget to do it right."

- "I hope you can pull it off this time."

- "Let me give you lots of advice on this assignment."

- "When you're more experienced, I'll let you do it."

- "I told you to be more careful, didn't I?"

- "Don't expect too much around here."

- "We've operated this way for so long and nothing will change."

- "This is a complicated project. Are you sure you can handle it?"

- "Well, do the best you can, I guess. OK?"

- "Hopefully, you'll be able to get it done properly."

There are numerous reasons individuals or groups of employees are discouraged. It could be the restrictive, bureaucracy-heavy, punishment-oriented culture of the organization, autocratic and oppressive management, demotivating rules and policies, lack of career advancement opportunities, conflict among groups, too much politics and favoritism, unavailability of interesting work assignments and projects, no rewards for excellence and achievements, work burnouts and a host of other reasons.

The symptoms of discouraged employees can be as countless and varied as the causes. Some signs that workers are disappointed, disheartened and even demoralized are they complain about being overwhelmed, and that work is enormously stressful and not fun in any way. They have a low opinion of overall management actions and behaviors. They say they never feel appreciated or valued and have stopped taking any extra initiative or volunteering ideas, solutions or recommendations to improve things. They do the minimum of what is asked of them, so their active engagement is low, and employee turnover is high. Numerous studies show that when employees are asked about the specific psychological issue of being discouraged people overwhelmingly point to the behavior of their managers as the determining factor.

Psychological Impact of Encouraging Others

Alfred Adler, a well-known Austrian psychotherapist, medical doctor and founder of Adlerian psychology, along with his followers, considered encouragement in therapy a crucial factor for human growth and development. He stated, "Altogether, in every step of treatment, we must not deviate from the path of encouragement." Those encouragement skills by a therapist during therapy (especially for those who were discouraged, demoralized or depressed by various life situations) included active listening, empathy, showing respect for and confidence in those patients, focusing on their assets, strengths and resources and helping them better focus on their efforts and progress. Even enabling them to see the humor in life experiences helped encourage them.

According to Adler, when we feel encouraged, we feel more capable and appreciated and are more likely to act in a connected and more cooperative way with others, especially with those who encourage us. Adlerian psychologist Rudolf Dreikurs actually considered the ability to encourage others to be the most important attribute in getting along with other people. Johann Wolfgang von Goethe, considered the greatest German literary figure of the modern era, waxed philosophic with this advice, "Correction does much, but encouragement does more." Every manager, executive and leader must remember this.

There was a story in one of leadership expert John Maxwell's books about an experiment where people were tested standing in a bucket of ice water. Putting ice in water makes it more painful (as opposed to just ice alone) to endure for even brief periods of time. If a person falls into cold water with a temperature of say, 50F (10C) in a lake, sea or ocean, for example, it can actually kill a person in less than a minute. So, just putting your hands or feet into ice water is painful to endure for even those short sprints of time.

In Maxwell's book, he talks about how people were evaluated to see just how long they could endure by standing in a bucket of this frigid water. A record was made of their durations. Then, they tested more people, but this time, they had someone standing next to them cheering and encouraging them on to stay in the bitterly cold water. When the results came in, it showed that the people with someone encouraging them persisted and endured the pain twice as long as those who had no encouragement!

In a 2002 *Journal of Sports Sciences* article, they highlighted a study of 28 participants "to determine the effects of frequency of verbal encouragement during exercise testing (on a treadmill)." Surprisingly, the main finding was that verbal encouragement ("Excellent!" and "Way to go!" and "Good Job!" and "Push it!") during maximum exercise testing significantly alters several metabolic and cardiovascular variables. The results showed that verbal encouragement intended to increase a person's maximum effort had produced profound effects on performance. Who doesn't want to feel more important? Performance and business coaches use encouragement to reinforce the right things and the things done right and it builds loyalty to the manager or leader and the organization. It bears repeating that encouragement is a quick, no-cost way to benefit employees with maximum results.

Tolerance and Even Encouragement of "Failure" is Vital During Major Innovation Challenges and Setbacks

Teams of innovators looking to create breakthroughs and quantum leaps in science, technology, processes, systems or products and services and other areas of endeavor know the disappointment and even despair in dealing with numerous — sometimes seemingly endless —failed attempts to achieve their very lofty goals. Promise gives way to distress and hardships. The greater the "disruptive innovation," the more the various risks involved and uncertainty of outcomes. Even those with a persevering, optimistic spirit will feel the painful sting and deflationary effects of frequent reversals or lack of any progress.

Mac Lake, a pastor and leadership developer advised, "See potential in people and give them specific encouragement. Speak into their lives! The higher belief I have in you, the higher belief you have in yourself." The art of encouragement from leaders and managers is that of giving hope and support, which are especially vital during tough projects and complex, drawn-out innovations. When hard times come and discouragement digs into the soul, those reassuring words of hope can keep people pressing on ever longer.

4. ENCOURAGING & MOTIVATING YOUR PEOPLE TO PEAK PERFORMANCE

IBM's Thomas Watson, Sr. once smartly said, "The fastest way to succeed is to double your failure rate. You can be discouraged by failure, or you can learn from it. So, go ahead and make mistakes, make all you can. Because, remember that's where you'll find success —on the far side of failure." More executives today accept and even embrace this seemingly contrary-to-good business practice viewpoint.

They understand what innovators have always known — that failure and learning valuable lessons from them are a necessary (however unwelcomed) prerequisite to doing what has not been done before. The concept of "Intelligent Fast Failure" is catching on. A business simply can't develop a breakthrough product or process if it's not willing to encourage risk-taking and gleaning something of importance from subsequent mistakes. We're not talking about accepting dumb, repeatable or irresponsible mistakes, but well-meaning, carefully thought-out approaches and proposed solutions that did not pan out for whatever unexpected reasons.

At UPS in their operations, you receive a daily report card. You see everything has a measure from the amount of time it takes a driver to walk to your front door and drop off a package (ring bell wait) to the time unloading a 53-foot trailer. Industrial engineers have tested and come up with standard times to get jobs done. More often than not, before I went home with my daily report card, the grade was failing. This amount of failure, however, built a high level of resiliency and persistence in me. It encouraged me to look for a different way to solve the problem the next day. Creativity!

While companies are accepting the necessity of setbacks, complications, mishaps and outright failures during innovation projects disruptive in nature—by way of compensating management policies, processes, and practices — it's an entirely different matter at the personal level. Everyone hates to "fail" or to be viewed as doing so. Those who push boundaries and have them shoved back assume (realistically or not) that they'll suffer embarrassment, loss of esteem, credibility and stature. And nowhere is the fear of failure more biting than in the competitive world of business, where a serious mistake might mean losing a bonus, a promotion, or even a job from a harsh, intolerant management.

As former CEO of Monsanto, Robert B. Shapiro saw just how unnerved and even terrified his employees were of failing. They had been naturally conditioned to see an unsuccessful new product development or project that fizzled as a personal stain on their performance and reputation. As a leader, Shapiro worked hard to change that emotional feeling and perception knowing it hindered the imaginative thinking, drive and initiative and the resulting innovation that fueled his chemical and biotechnology business.

He emphasized to his employees that every new product, project and process development was simply an experiment or test. He said that teams failed only if their work was a halfhearted, careless effort giving poor results without learning something from it. But an intentional, deliberate, well-thought-out creative effort that didn't succeed was not only excusable but also desirable as they would get valuable information from it that would benefit that project or others that came later. He strived to encourage his employees to reach far out in exploration of radical ideas, knowing that only a small-to-moderate percentage of them would yield impressive fruit.

Such a positive attitude and approach to making intelligent mistakes in the pursuit of big gains is characteristic of people I call "smart-fault-tolerant leaders"— exceptional executives who, through their encouraging and supportive words and actions, help people overcome their negative fear of failure and, in the process, craft a culture of necessary risk-taking that leads to on-going innovation breakthroughs that other organizations shy away from. These rare and transcendent leaders don't just accept learning-based failure, they encourage it and even praise it as a courageous badge of honor.

4. ENCOURAGING & MOTIVATING YOUR PEOPLE TO PEAK PERFORMANCE

Pygmalion Effect Can Encourage and Promote Exceptional, Unexpected Results

There are those who can and those who can't, those who will and those who won't. Managers are fortunate to have those who believe they can and will do things that others can't or won't. The fascinating *Pygmalion effect* (also called the *Rosenthal effect*) is a phenomenon ideal to strongly encourage and support those types of results-oriented and optimistic people. The effect even works with those who want to do well but may not seem to be as confident and secure in themselves as others. The Pygmalion effect applies and is beneficial to numerous people in various situations such as sports teams, students, entertainers, artists, military professionals, academics and basically those in most kinds of fields of endeavor in organizations and corporations.

As a leader, when you hold and communicate positive expectations toward individual employees or team members, this proven psychological effect can lead to better performance and superior achievements that might even astound both you and them. The flipside of the Pygmalion effect is the *Golem effect*, where low expectations, pessimistic discussions and outlooks, frequent criticisms and demeaning of someone will lead to decreases in performance, sometimes severe in nature. For example, in one simple study, when researchers remind elderly people that cognition typically declines with age, they perform worse on memory tests than those who had no such reminder. Either way, we get the outcomes and behaviors we expect. It's a "self-fulfilling" prophecy. When our (especially strong) beliefs and presumptions influence our behavior at the powerful subconscious level, we are enacting that self-fulfilling prophecy. Psychologists discovered strong evidence for the direct impact these thoughts have on actual outcomes, especially when we are convinced that our predictions will happen, even when we aren't directly aware that we hold that expectation.

Interestingly, the name of this effect comes from the story by the Roman poet Ovid of a mythical Greek sculptor Pygmalion who was also the King of Cypress. In the story, he intricately carved an incredibly life-like and stunningly beautiful statue of his ideal woman out of ivory. He became so smitten and emotionally overwhelmed with his creation, that he spent all his time gazing upon his perfection and then fell in love with it. Pygmalion made offerings at the altar of Aphrodite, the goddess of love and begged her to bring his statue to life, which she did. His dream, his extraordinary high expectations and unshakeable belief that his stature of unsurpassed beauty could come to life as he imagined became a self-fulfilling prophecy.

The social psychologist Robert Rosenthal and Lenore Jacobson originally used the *Pygmalion effect* term to describe the fascinating and unmistakable results of a landmark experiment they carried out in 1965 in a California school that confirmed the potency and effectiveness of the self-fulfilling prophecy. Students in a California elementary school were given an IQ test as part of the beginning study. Scores were not disclosed to teachers. Teachers were told that about 20 percent of the students (selected completely at random) were likely gifted "intellectual bloomers" and that they were expected to perform academically better compared to their more "average" classmates. Teachers were given the names of pupils thought to be intellectually superior. Amazingly, these students showed a significantly greater gain in performance over their classmates when tested again at the end of the year. The *only* difference between these students and their peers, Rosenthal wrote, "was in the mind of the teacher" and how that teacher behaved toward them. Key findings from this experiment (and other subsequent ones like it) proved that teacher expectations of students influenced their performance *more* than any differences in talent or intelligence!

How do elevated expectations promote this greater achievement? Rosenthal found that higher, positive expectations caused teachers to act differently regarding the learners by developing a warmer, more supportive climate for and relationship with students they regarded as more prone to excelling. More smiles, nodding and touches on the shoulders were ways to build stronger relationships. In addition, teachers spent more time to answer questions and engage students more in discussions.

The teachers also gave these "elite learners" more specific, comprehensive and personal feedback on their academic work, not just an abstract "good job" or "well done." As Rosenthal summed it up, "When we expect certain behaviors of others, we are likely to act in ways that make the expected behavior more likely to occur." Back in the 19th century, French journalist and best-selling novelist Anatole France might have known that when he said, "Nine-tenths of education is encouragement." Sometimes it's difficult to deliberately change our expectations of others. However, we can consciously change our behavior and how we communicate with others, including employees.

A self-fulfilling prophecy can play out with employees assigned a new project or task that the people initially feel is outside of their perceived ability and expertise. They might think to themselves, "There's no way I can do this. I'm bound to falter and fail." The employees might then unconsciously put less emotional and mental effort into the project, thinking it's a lost cause. They might avoid taking risks, learning new things and asking others for assistance since they believe the project is doomed anyway. When the project falls flat, they likely think, "See, I was right, I knew and believed I just couldn't succeed" without realizing that their attitude, perceptions and behavior all but guaranteed that the project would fail.

What are the implications for leaders, executives and managers in all kinds of organizations and industries? Tel Aviv University professor Dov Eden has demonstrated the Pygmalion effect in numerous work environments and situations. He confirmed that if those in authority and leadership positions hold positive, high expectations about the performance of those they lead, believing they can solve complex, seemingly insurmountable problems and achieve innovations (especially those of a breakthrough or disruptive kind), then individual or team performance will significantly improve and extraordinary results will blossom. On the other hand, if the leader holds negative, pessimistic expectations – believing and (directly or indirectly) communicating that the group will not do well — it will lead to performance declines and perhaps even drastically poor results — the dreaded Golem effect. Regarding the Pygmalion effect, Dov Eden says, "it sounds so simple. It seems too good to be true." Yet, competent and sincere use of it by those in charge shows it to be true and effective.

How to Uplift, Motivate and Build Confidence Using the Pygmalion Effect in Communication and Actions

The positive language you use and how you act with confidence and genuine high expectations toward your employees are critical in getting superior performance from them. Here are two examples in which a leader can communicate that positive results are likely to happen. Notice the wording for the intended psychological impact on the people receiving the spoken part of the Pygmalion effect. Some managers or leaders would tone down the language and de-tune the superlatives in these examples and not use such strong verbal "pats-on-the-back" that may not work with some individuals and teams. But you get the idea of what the goal is to broadcast high expectations and a hoped-for self-fulfilling prophecy of actions and outcomes with these examples.

Example 1:

"I personally hired each of you engineers because you have exceptional educations and skills, diverse and valuable experiences in a number of unique areas, proven problem-solving abilities and a drive to continuously out-innovate our products and manufacturing processes compared to our best competitors. I consider this team to be among the very best in the industry. I expect you to excel in the three challenging, exciting projects in which you will be working over the next 18 months. There are incredibly demanding requirements you will be asked to fulfill and you will be immersed in tough, vexing problems unlike anything you've faced before.

4. ENCOURAGING & MOTIVATING YOUR PEOPLE TO PEAK PERFORMANCE

There will be seemingly insurmountable technical obstacles that will thwart you and you'll very likely experience disappointing, unnerving setbacks, simply because you are pushing the absolute boundaries of technology and engineering and doing what others won't even attempt. If anyone will succeed, it is your highly capable, creative team of super-innovators. I have absolute faith in your achieving these radically over-the-top goals! You will have my total support in every aspect throughout this adventure."

The Pygmalion effect can be used on people who might otherwise feel somewhat less qualified or unworthy for a major endeavor. Assuming you have total confidence in their ability to accomplish it, you can say something like the following to encourage them. Notice how the manager "justifies" her decision and decisively and strongly communicates it.

Example 2:

"I'm promoting you to Director of Advanced Material Sciences in charge of leading the development of new composites and materials for our aerospace customers. While you say you have had less experience in this area and being a bit of a perfectionist, you expressed you are not quite ready for this next step in your career, I disagree! I know you are ready and able to assume the position and excel at it because you have a PhD with an impressive thesis in this technical arena, you've already successfully worked on five new material breakthroughs and you've written four technical papers that were outstanding in opening new scientific grounds in metal-to-ceramic super materials. Your team has total faith in having you assume this leadership role and so do I! You're one the quickest learners I've had the pleasure to work with. I would not jeopardize my position here promoting you if I felt the least bit of concern or doubt. You're ready, you're able, you're our new Director. Congratulations!"

Canadian broadcaster and playwright Lister Sinclair profoundly said, "A frightened captain makes a frightened crew." The same psychology applies to a manager wrongly applying the Pygmalion effect. If your body language or tone of voice or general actions and behaviors appear tentative, doubtful, reluctant, hesitant or timid in how you are attempting to encourage people, the person receiving it will not believe it. You have to believe it most of all, and it will come across that way.

Power of Praise, Recognition and Rewards to Impact Performance

When a leader uses effective praise, recognition and rewards, it creates positive emotions that have rippling effects throughout an organization. Unfortunately, many employees complain that their managers are remiss in doling out well-deserved acknowledgment, appreciation and compliments for good work — or even for extraordinary achievements. According to the U.S. Department of Labor, the number one reason people leave their jobs is because they "do not feel appreciated." Simple, quick and warranted praise and recognition are the least expensive, quickest and easiest to do leadership behaviors that give impressive, proven returns on investment of time and effort. Successful managers know that they can give an abundance of recognition if it's genuine, specific and earned. Acknowledging an employee's best work goes a long way toward making him or her feel truly appreciated and valued and will lead to other desirable workplace outcomes.

According to a Gallup analysis, only one in three workers in the U.S. strongly agree that they received praise or recognition for doing a good job in the past seven days. Data shows that it's not uncommon for employees to feel that their best efforts are not just periodically, but routinely ignored. Employees who do not feel adequately recognized are twice as likely to voice that they'll quit in the next year. This surprising lack of acknowledging improved work practices, accomplishments and professionalism, for example, and not giving compliments and praise might be one of the greatest missed opportunities for leaders and managers to boost employee engagement to the company that leads to improved retention.

Whether you call it encouragement, praise, acknowledgment or recognition, when a person in power or influence gives it to a person, it activates a powerful brain chemical—a neurotransmitter—called *dopamine* in the individual receiving positive feedback or reinforcement. Dopamine produces positive emotions like pride, pleasure, happiness, satisfaction, motivation, concentration and even bliss under certain conditions. When employees experience an extended period of reduction in this brain chemical, work is impaired (to various degrees) by performance-limiting emotions of frustration, anxiety, boredom, resentment and lack of motivation. Using encouraging praise can boost dopamine that sustains individuals and teams during difficult and energy-sapping projects, especially those of an innovative nature where setbacks, complications and resistance from others are impeding progress.

During another Gallup workplace survey, employees were asked to cite who gave them their most consequential and unforgettable recognition. Interesting results disclosed that the most memorable and impacting recognition they received came from their manager (28 percent), followed by a prominent leader or CEO (24 percent), the manager's manager (12 percent), a customer (10 percent) and peers (9 percent) while "other" was cited by the remaining 17 percent. What's most intriguing about these findings? Nearly one-quarter said the most memorable recognition comes from a person in a high-level position. Employees will greatly remember and be emotionally affected by a personal remark or congratulations from the CEO or other important executive. Even a seemingly small gesture from a high-ranking leader to show appreciation can make a significant impression (perhaps even a career highlight) on an employee.

How to Best Recognize and Praise People for Maximum Motivation and Encouragement

It's important to identify those behaviors and skills that need to be encouraged so your organization can better meet your goals and operating standards of excellence. I've discovered that a one-size-fits-all encouraging approach to boosting the dopamine in my employees doesn't work. Everyone is different in that some people love a public display of appreciation and recognition, whether in front of others or in the organization's newsletter or social media. Others like a quiet, subdued and personal, one-on-one display of praise. Even a written thank you note can be effective. And while regular monthly or quarterly acts of formal recognition are useful, I recommend even daily forms of simple praise when you catch someone doing something right or worthy of special attention. Get to know how each of your employees prefer to be recognized and tailor and personalize how you praise and honor them. And be careful about praising behaviors, skills and achievements that come way too easy to employees. They might perceive that as uncalled for, insincere and even gratuitous.

When I was the head of HR for the City of Houston, and now in my executive position in Harris Health System, I would be on alert to regularly praise something from as many of my employees as possible. The key is to be specific and genuine and brief in doing it — and not overdoing it. For example, I might compliment a manager for how she coached her direct report by saying something like:

"At our weekly meeting, I really liked the way you coached Marcus. You highlighted and congratulated him on the extra effort and hard work he did on the health insurance cost reduction report and the improved quality of his analysis and recommendations. I saw his face light up from your enthusiastic compliment. By giving him specific, positive feedback, he will continue to improve and do great work. Thank you for your leadership and professionalism!"

Sometimes a brief acknowledgment goes a long way, even if you are just passing in the hallway together. A while back, I said this to one of my talented trainers, "I heard you and your team brainstormed some bold ideas to boost innovation in our operations. I can't wait to hear about them. I love that you're pushing the envelope, instead of playing it safe with mediocre ideas." Communicating you recognize someone's extra effort and dedication (not just achievement or results) is valuable too such as saying, "Karla, I see you spending extra evenings here and I heard you've put in some long weekends wrapping up our HR Mindfulness Workshop to ensure we get it done on time and on target. I appreciate your extra effort. It did not go unnoticed by me. Thank you so much!" Even a brief, "Brianna, third time you reduced operating costs this quarter in your department. Bravo! Let me take you and your team to lunch next week to celebrate, OK?"

It's estimated that American companies spend between 1-2 percent of payroll on recognition rewards (such as gifts like watches, plaques, trips, gift cards, pins) that surprisingly amounts to over $45 billion, but analysis shows most of these recognition programs focus on tenure, not on performance or accomplishments. One study found that companies in the top 20 percent of having a "recognition-rich culture" had a 31 percent reduced (voluntary) turnover rate. Companies that value recognition make it easy and frequent to do across all areas of operations and many link their recognition and rewards to their organization's goals and values. Some also include their recognition and reward policies based on creative ideas generated and innovations and improvements produced. The book *1501 Ways to Reward Employees* by Bob Nelson will give you lots of good ideas, many of which are imaginative, inexpensive and quick to do.

Motivated Employees Are Fully Engaged, Productive and Creative

The term "morale" is often used interchangeably with "motivation." Both are important to a positive and productive workplace, yet they are different. Morale is an emotional and mental condition and feeling exhibited by feeling happy, satisfied, confident, optimistic and secure on the job. Employees enjoy being there at work. They may like their pay and benefits, overall working conditions, the cafeteria at work, resources available, nice office décor, the organizational culture and supportive management. With high morale, employees are keen to come to work and have a positive attitude and are more inclined to work harder and produce a higher level and quality of work.

When morale sinks, workers become less motivated, less engaged and simply "go through the motions." There are exceptions where highly motivated people do great work, even if their morale and that of others in the organization is low, perhaps because they love the project or activity they're involved in and have high professional and personal standards to do their best regardless. Having high morale is generally a good thing, but it does not necessarily mean that people are motivated and driven to excel on the job and willing to deal with difficult situations, challenges or problems.

The word motivation stems from the Latin word "movere" which means to move, to behave and act in some way. A motive is a stimulus for action and is why we do things rather than what or how we do it. When motivated, it energizes and causes us toward a goal. There are two main types of motivation: intrinsic and extrinsic. *Extrinsic motivation* is being motivated to behave, perform a task or engage in an activity to earn a reward or to avoid punishment.

You do it not because you enjoy it or because you find it satisfying for its own sake, but to get something in return or avoid something unpleasant or undesirable. *Intrinsic motivation* involves doing something because it is personally rewarding, satisfying, enjoyable or fun. You do it because you want to, not have to do it. Employees who are highly engaged in the job find themselves intrinsically (or self) motivated. For example, people who love being creative have this self-driven type of motivation.

Here are just some ways to help motivate your employees:

1. Inject some fun and competition into work. Consider introducing elements of gameplay where people and teams win medals, fun trophies and small gifts. Friendly competition that varies each month helps engage individuals and teams. About two years ago, I gave out an annual award to the best team. This group of people worked most collaboratively, showed high morale, motivation and smoked the expected results.

4. ENCOURAGING & MOTIVATING YOUR PEOPLE TO PEAK PERFORMANCE

2. Eliminate as many demotivating factors at work as possible. That would make a huge difference!

3. Discover what your people need and want to do and see if you can give them assignments and projects well suited for their skills and likes.

4. Provide sufficient resources and support to help them succeed and accomplish the results to which they would be proud.

5. Give people as much autonomy, decision-making and ownership over their jobs as possible and warranted.

6. Provide and support a clear path to career advancement or escalating rewards for doing excellent work.

7. Give them challenging tasks and projects and "stretch goals" where employees can feel a sense of satisfaction in achieving them and where they can use their creativity to solve problems, bring about improvements and make a real difference on the job.

8. Within your organization, promote an optimistic, "can do" attitude.

9. Celebrate wins and successes by individuals and teams. Do it regularly to put more enjoyment and fun in work.

10. Hear their ideas, suggestions, feelings, complaints or anything else they are interested in or concerned about. Then take as quick and decisive action as possible whenever it is beneficial and warranted.

11. Don't ignore problems in the workplace. Whether it is dealing with underperforming employees who affect others, low morale, increasing obstacles to getting things done or anything else, deal with it to avoid it getting out of hand.

12. Take the initiative and regularly ask for their advice, input and feedback to give them a full opportunity to express and vent themselves.

13. Always treat people with the dignity and respect they deserve. Never put them on the spot, embarrass them or otherwise belittle them, even in the slightest way. You will lose their trust, respect and loyalty. Make them feel important and needed.

14. Schedule one-on-one time with as many people as you can to build rapport and strengthen relationships with those you lead. Provide coaching and feedback and support for their performance goals.

15. As a leader, role model the values and ethics you are striving to embed and instill in your followers or employees.

One Important Strategy is to STOP Demotivating People

W. Edwards Deming was considered the leader and father of Total Quality Management (TQM) and was greatly responsible for helping Japan attain industrial and manufacturing excellence and dominance after World War Two. He repeatedly chastised managers for actions and behaviors that wrecked the motivation and morale of workers, "If management stopped demotivating their employees, then they wouldn't have to worry so much about motivating them." When there is no feedback on the positive aspects of work and only negative feedback given, for example, it saps the energy, enthusiasm and engagement of people. As a result, organizations suffer from the impact of poor leadership.

I tell leaders that most employees don't get up daily, prepare for work at home, use transportation, get to work, clock in, speak with co-workers and then decide they want to fail. Most people want to succeed. Leaders must remove obstacles that keep their people from succeeding. Part of my job is "Chief Obstacle Remover."

Managers are fortunate to have intrinsically motivated and engaged employees who will do a great job if they are not repeatedly hindered by an organization's bureaucratic red tape and unnecessarily rigid rules and policies that impede creativity, productivity and efficiency. Remove the things and bad management behaviors that demotivate people and see what happens.

A demotivated person will stop volunteering for new projects, avoid taking any initiative at work and show no interest in attending training programs or workshops. They will likely complain a lot and spread negativity and pessimism ("Why bother?") to others. Absenteeism will increase, and frequent employee turnover is a sign people are unhappy, frustrated and convinced that things will not get better (but probably worse) on the job. Studies show that the main reason people "jump ship" is because of their direct manager that they feel is a poor leader and someone who (directly or indirectly) thwarts their career advancement and work satisfaction.

I don't believe a vast majority of managers purposely set out to demotivate their people. But, too many are unaware of their behaviors and policies that impede performance. I know that because executives and managers are stressed out with huge workloads and other priorities and challenges that they often inadvertently miss opportunities to do the things needed by their people and are not cognizant of the demotivating factors operating under the surface festering in their organizations.

Here are just some common management actions — or lack of them — that will negatively affect morale and motivation:

1. **Poor communications and lack of clear directions.** In a recent Interact/Harris poll of 1,000 employees, 91 percent said that communicating well was a critical skill their leaders lacked and 57 percent mentioned that they were not given clear directions for work-related activities. Teamwork and morale took a hit as a result, according to the survey respondents.

2. **Fuzzy job expectations.** If employees don't know what success in their jobs look like and are unsure of the exact roles and responsibilities, they have to do excellent work in which to excel, their outlook and temperament will suffer over time. They must understand the priorities they should focus on

during each month or sooner. This lack of clarity can confuse and frustrate people.

3. **Micromanaging.** Even if a manager has good intentions of helping and guiding employees in the work, by hovering over them, constantly telling them what to do and how to do it and making practically all decisions for them, it will sap the life out of people. It will chase away top talent, kill their drive, creativity, problem-solving and ownership of situations. Not empowering people and having them always wait for approval and sign off from managers for the littlest things will put their motivation firmly in reverse gear.

4. **Having a lot of useless, stupid rules.** All organizations need necessary rules to be organized, efficient and productive. However, when employees have to deal with rigid, foolish or unfair rules and policies that make no common sense, but, instead, put an unnecessary burden on them and restrict their ability to perform and enjoy work, that greatly affects morale, motivation and drive. I once read that rules don't govern human progress, they govern human past. They usually follow, not lead behavior.

5. **Undervaluing people.** If employees feel that their efforts and achievements are not being recognized, appreciated and rewarded, they'll lack the energy, initiative and commitment to sustain a high level of performance. Taking people for granted without giving them positive feedback and acknowledgment is highly demotivating. In that Interact/Harris poll of 1,000 employees, 63 percent of them reported that their managers did not recognize (let alone reward and appreciate) their achievements.

6. **Being apathetic.** Most people who leave their jobs do so because of their relationship (or lack of) with their boss. Managers who show no care, compassion, understanding or empathy for their employees will always have high turnover rates.

7. **Ruling by fear and intimidation.** Some managers believe that things cannot get done properly unless they maintain constant control and threaten

or intimidate workers to do exactly as the manager "ordered." Who wants to work with a fear-based manager who creates a climate of anxiety, stress and negativity? No one is likely to be honest about problems or bring up new ideas or proposed solutions for fear of being attacked, punished or fired.

8. **Making unreasonable demands and being inconsistent.** If employees feel that their workload and performance standards are way out of reach and unreasonable, their morale will plummet. How can people be motivated and productive when they have to work late into the evening and at home on the weekends (particularly when a project is not critical and time-sensitive)? When people feel that their manager is asking them to do the truly impossible, they become anxious or numb and demotivated. Holding employees to a high standard (as I discussed previously) is a very good thing, but crossing the line into outrageous, unachievable demands is another. Also, if a manager constantly changes his or her mind on directions, expectations and other work criteria for no apparent or logical reason, it causes stressful "dissonance" that will affect performance and quality of work.

9. **Not following through on commitments.** Employees take a manager's executive's commitments very seriously. When we as leaders uphold commitments we've made and honor even small promises, we become trustworthy and honorable in the eyes of our followers and employees, two very important qualities in a leader. When managers frequently and nonchalantly disregard what they said they would do, employee motivation to go above and beyond their job descriptions will crash.

10. **Being disinterested in them personally.** When a manager or leader simply sees people are interchangeable, faceless cogs in a wheel, as dispensable and replaceable, there is no personal relationship built and nurtured. Managers who fail to learn even a little about their people — their families, backgrounds, needs and wants on the job, hobbies and outside interests — will lose an opportunity to bond with them and gain their loyalty and even affection.

11. **Disregarding or shooting down ideas.** One of the best ways to demotivate and disengage employees is to consistently be unresponsive, closed-minded or worse yet outwardly critical to new ideas, proposed solutions or any recommendation they bring up. If a manager at least openly listens and preferably encourages the staff to participate and offer ways to improve things, people will be more motivated on the job.

12. **Boring work.** Let's face it, not all jobs are satisfying, let along fun, glamorous or exciting. Most of us would love to have challenging, psychologically rewarding and fulfilling jobs where we feel we are making a real difference. A recent article in the Huffington Post revealed that 55 percent of Generation X and Generation Y workers believe that finding a job personally gratifying is worth sacrifices in salary. Even if managers must get creative to put variety and spark in their groups' jobs, they could put a big dent in reducing demotivated employees.

Omar's Bright Ideas

Summary for You to Make a Difference by Encouraging and Motivating People

1. Ask yourself how often you actually encourage people on a regular basis and think about how you encourage them and the impact it has.

2. Poll your employees about what specifically motivates them and get their ideas and recommendations to ensure they are primed for success.

3. Find out all the possible things that demotivate your followers and employees from doing their very best and see if you can fix or eliminate as many of those demotivators as possible.

4. Work at becoming proficient using the Pygmalion effect, especially during innovation-related projects or other challenging activities and tasks that cause people to somewhat doubt their ability to successfully finish them.

4. ENCOURAGING & MOTIVATING YOUR PEOPLE TO PEAK PERFORMANCE

5.   Put together a plan and strategy on how to better motivate your employees or followers, understanding that you may have to tailor and personalize your approaches to energize an individual's (or team's) work performance.

6.   Always be on the lookout to privately or publicly recognize, praise and compliment (according to each person's preference) their accomplishments or even small improvements in that employee's performance.

7.   Identify the reasons some employees might be discouraged (not necessarily demotivated) at work and take adequate actions to overcome them.

8.   Put together a reward system for your employees that involves both monetary and non-monetary rewards for exceptional work.

M.A.D.* LEADERSHIP

Chapter 5

M.A.D. Leaders Are Great Listeners
Your Soft Skills of Listening and Questioning Will Get You Hard Results

"Listening is a master skill for personal and professional greatness."
– Robin S. Sharma

You may think it unusual, but this chapter about listening and asking questions is one of the most important as it relates to being an effective manager, team member and certainly a leader. I learned a long time ago that if you are to retain talented people and get the best performance from them, you must *really* listen to them — to their ideas, opinions, recommendations, plans, strategies, solutions, and overall feedback. In addition, because leadership deals in the world of emotions and feelings, a leader must sincerely and empathically listen to their problems, disappointments, frustrations, insecurities, grievances, fears, concerns, dissatisfactions and complaints so you can help to resolve those that affect their work and to show you genuinely care about their welfare and feelings. At those times, your title and mine might be "Chief Listening Officer." Listening is a skill you definitely should want to be great at. A recent study conducted at George Washington University showed that listening can influence up to 40 percent of a leader's job performance.

I try to spend my time as Senior VP of HR at Harris Health System not just on transactional HR issues, but strategic and transformational ones with more impact on operational quality, culture and innovation. You can't achieve meaningful change without the enthusiastic and eager engagement of your staff. When a leader frequently and actively listens and asks smart probing questions of them to solve problems and explore opportunities, people are more willing to make a difference at work. They get engaged. Improvements happen. Innovations begin to sprout all over.

I tell the story of my time as HR Director for the City of Houston. Coming from the private sector I had limited knowledge of municipal government. So, during my first 120 days on the job, I went on a "listening tour" of the 24 departments before I started to implement any changes. I spoke with employees and leaders from all levels of the organization and gained a valuable understanding of what needed to improve immediately and what could remain the same. When I talk with new hires, I tell them about the importance of being a good listener. I talk about when I started dating my wife 28 years ago. We've been married for 26 years now. If I wanted the relationship initially to succeed, I had to discover what was important to her. How did she want to be treated and how was I going to impress her? Understanding her favorite color (gray), her favorite movie (*It's a Wonderful Life*), her favorite food (fried chicken).

How Would You Feel?

Suppose you were at a business networking event or social affair and you meet and introduce yourself to that person. You quickly find out that he is charming, charismatic, and a delightful "conversationalist" who is regaling you with his fascinating stories and insights on various topics, right from the start. You don't mind his non-stop talking about himself and sharing his feelings and opinions because he is very interesting and obviously knows his stuff, even though he has asked nothing about you. It's enjoyable listening to him.

A few minutes later, you then meet another person who is warm and cordial and who totally engages you from the get-go. She wants to know about you and your job. She seems very interested in *you* from a professional standpoint and asks your opinions on a number of areas in which you are involved at work. She nods her head and smiles a lot at your answers and focuses all her attention on you. This person seems to hang onto every word of yours. She hardly talks about herself. Instead, she's enthralled with listening to you, especially about this creative idea you are sharing with her about a new social media marketing campaign at work.

You suddenly become aware that you are doing all the talking, but you're emotionally sucked into it without being able to stop the one-sided talking on your part taking place. What a "delightful listener," you think! She apparently took to heart the famous publisher and entrepreneur Malcolm Forbe's maxim, "The art of conversation lies in listening." Now, who would you generally prefer to spend time with — a terrific talker who takes and hogs the spotlight, or a great listener who puts the spotlight on you? You know the answer. It's been said that listening is the sincerest form of flattery. Stephen Covey, the author of the highly popular book, *The 7 Habits of Highly Effective People,* noted, "When you really listen to another person from their point of view, and reflect back to them that understanding, it's like giving them emotional oxygen."

The next day at work, you're stoked about your idea because this intelligent woman, who apparently had a lot of business experience and savvy (based upon the little she shared about herself), validated it. You excitedly go into your manager's office to tell him about it. He's texting on his phone and says, "Go ahead, tell me about this idea. I can multi-task. He doesn't look at you while he's texting away. Suddenly, someone comes into his office and he abruptly switches attention and starts talking with that person. After about four minutes of disregarding you, he blurts out, "Go ahead with your idea!" You continue while he looks at his computer screen to read a detailed email he just received.

Shortly afterward, he seems impatient and distracted and says, "How long will it take for you to finish telling me about this? I've got a lot to work on today." You reply, "No problem. I'll tell you about it later." You thought *maybe* this time with this big idea of yours, he would listen. Dejectedly, you've resigned yourself not to try again. You finally conclude that your boss does, in fact, have the attention span and interest of a ferret on a double espresso.

In an Interact/Harris poll that was highlighted in a 2015 Harvard Business Review article, "The Top Complaints from Employees About Their Leaders," 91 percent of employees identified communication issues as a serious pain point with their managers. "Not having time to meet with employees" was cited by 52 percent of the survey respondents as a lack of effective leadership from their bosses. In 1999, the U.S. Department of Labor statistics revealed that 46 percent of people who ultimately quit their jobs did so because they felt they were not listened to and were therefore unappreciated.

If Communication Is a Good Part of Our Day, We Ought to Do It Well

One of my favorite authors and speakers is John Maxwell. He wrote a book titled, *Everyone Communicates, Few Connect.* In my many leadership roles over the years, I have had the opportunity to meet many influential people. The ones who left the greatest impression are the ones who listened to me. Subscribers to the *Harvard Business Review* rated the ability to communicate the most important fact in making an executive promotable — more important than ambition, education and even hard work.

The number one quality HR executives like myself want is effective communication skills from new hires that determines so many aspects of good job performance and ability to get along with others. Studies show that in 7 out of 10 minutes during most of our time, we communicate with another person. In a typical business day on average, we spend about 45 percent of our time listening, 30 percent of our time talking, 16 percent reading and 9 percent writing. The ones who do it right, usually get ahead faster in their career than others.

Even though listening is our primary communication activity, a great majority of us listen at only about a 25 percent comprehension rate! That's because listening is a very difficult behavior and skill to master. It's much more than just about hearing or being able to feedback the words a person is telling us. Only about 2 percent of all professionals have had formal education or training to improve listening skills and techniques.

5. M.A.D. LEADERS ARE GREAT LISTENERS

So much emphasis in business communication is placed on giving a convincing, compelling and get-results presentation. Of course, being a polished and powerful public speaker and presenter is a considerable leadership skill to have, no doubt. But listening is as important and sometimes more so because of the significant benefits it gives the listener and person speaking. Let's face it, you can be a dynamic, mesmerizing speaker who is an "oral flamethrower," but if you are a poor listener, it can greatly detract from your otherwise respected persona and even sink your professional and personal effectiveness. "Silent" has the same letters as "listen," but the act of good listening is so much more than just being passive. As you know from your experience, most people don't listen intending to understand, they listen intending to reply as soon as an opening in the conversation occurs. Your ears will never get you into trouble as former U.S. President Calvin Coolidge testified, "No man ever listened himself out of a job."

Perceptions About A Leader With "Good" Or "Bad" Listening Skills

Years ago, in the television business, they had a saying that "Perception is reality" and when it comes to judging how a person listens, that's generally true. Perception is a mental impression of someone or something — how one interprets things. When people experience being with a manager, business executive or leader who is an exceptionally good listener, that person will "project" an image he or she is likely to have some combination of the following positive traits based upon the type of meaningful conversations and good listening you have from the leader:

Trustworthy	Open-minded	Competent	Thoughtful
Tactful	Empathic	Sensitive	Self-controlled
Friendly	Cooperative	Relaxed	Fair-minded
Reasonable	Conscientious	Intelligent	Likable
Sincere	Secure	Considerate	Authentic

Selfless   Caring   Ethical   Honest

Dependable Imaginative   Adaptable   Compassionate

Accepting   Non-judgmental   Responsible Confident

Now, suppose you meet and spend some time with a high-level manager who speed-talks in full-blown monologue mode, dominating the conversation with his strong beliefs and ideas, has no eye contact with you, constantly looks at his phone while you find brief talk time, frequently interrupts you, or jumps in to tell you of his situation or story and neglects to respond to your thoughts or feelings on what is being "discussed."

I remember the first time I interacted with a high-level leader, who communicated through what I call a "stream of consciousness thinking." His team was used to it and reacted like it was no big deal. I remember after the meeting asking someone, "Was this how all the meetings were conducted?" When they said yes, I came up with a different plan on how to spend my time during the meeting — like not attending.

Would you perceive and describe this poor listener as having some mix of the following negative character traits?

Inconsiderate	Rigid	Intolerant	Aggressive
Tactless	Selfish	Close-minded	Inflexible
Nervous	Thoughtless	Immature	Boring
Self-centered	Insecure	Impulsive	Superficial
Defensive	Stubborn	Disrespectful	Boorish
Unreliable	Oblivious	Impatient	Opinionated
Judgmental	Controlling	Uncooperative	Petty
Untrustworthy	Shallow	Shortsighted	Unappreciative

5. M.A.D. LEADERS ARE GREAT LISTENERS

Being a good or bad listener doesn't necessarily mean that a person actually has any of those traits listed. But amazingly, being a great listener projects such a positive image of a person that people somehow believe and feel those traits, characteristics and behaviors are "attached" and belong to a manager, executive or leader. Likewise, being a terrible listener causes people to view a person in a harsh light. Whether right or wrong, listening skills are like a psychological and emotional barometer that will measure and brand a person's credibility, reputation and leadership image accordingly. Bernard Baruch, the famous financier, statesman, and political consultant, summed it up very simply, "Most of the successful people I've known are the ones who do more listening than talking."

Why Effective Listening is Very Tough

A lot of us think that just remaining quiet, trying to understand what someone is saying and asking relevant questions is good listening. Well, that's certainly a start. Intense listening can be very taxing on a person's ability to focus and concentrate. We typically talk at the rate of between 120 to 180 words per minute, but we think at the high rate of between 1,000 to 3,000 words per minute. So, the natural tendency with this huge "mental processing free time" is to be distracted and not listen attentively for extended periods, especially if we find the person or topic being covered to be boring, too complex, or not relevant to us.

Whether we consciously know it or not, we also listen through "filters" that can distort or color how we interpret what someone is saying. They include things like the experiences we've had and knowledge we've accumulated, the assumptions you are making about a person or the topic being discussed, listening to someone with a difficult-to-understand accent, your own needs during the conversation that are not being met, your strongly-held values, attitudes and beliefs about the topic you are hearing about, and your attention span and mental distractions. Add in expectations and biases you have during your listening activity, and you can see it's not easy to emotionally, comfortably and accurately perform listening. How we listen through these filters determine how successful we deal with the topic and person speaking.

BIG Benefits of Listening for a Leader

Most of the successful people I have known over my career and life do more listening than talking. I've discovered there are a multitude of important reasons to become a better listener. Wilson Mizner, an American playwright, raconteur and entrepreneur aptly said, "A good listener is not only popular everywhere, but after a while, he gets to know something." How true! Here are some other leadership benefits and advantages you can gain by being a better listener:

One: Builds Your Positive, Impressive Image. In the previous section, I listed all the positive traits and characteristics that people believe are part of the makeup of a great listener — that makes a great leader. Interestingly, when you combine good listening with a number of other key social behaviors like smiling and being engaging, people see you as being more charismatic! Because listening is a truly "magnetic quality," it draws people to the good listener. Who doesn't want to be around someone deeply interested in us and our thoughts, feelings and stories and who affirms our opinions and ideas and gives us encouraging feedback that says, "Keep talking. I love listening to you!" In that regard, it's an integral part of the charisma formula for the leader who listens. People respect good listeners and want to be around them because so few really exist! It's even surprising how many people perceive really good listeners as "smart," perhaps smarter than most managers and professionals at their workplace.

Two: Strengthens Relationships and Builds Trust. Ever wonder how even introverts and those who closely guard their feelings and secrets will disclose their innermost hurts, fears, insecurities and deep misgivings to a psychologist, therapist or psychiatrist —sometimes during the first session they have with that professional? One reason is they believe this person has a professional code and ethics to be discreet and not disclose anything about the patient. Also, these professionals are highly trained in empathic listening and questioning techniques with the goal of caring for and helping that troubled and hurting person. Trust is quickly built because the therapist, for example, is not judging the person even when he or she talks about situations that might otherwise shock or dismay others and cause a loss of respect for the person talking as a result. The more a therapist or psychiatrist listens intently with a deep concentration and focus, the more the patient reveals. The emotional and information disclosure faucet opens fully … and flows.

When a leader or executive emulates that type of deep listening with caring, empathy, non-judgment and openness to what that person is saying, then trust, and a rapport between the leader and that individual begins to develop and strengthen. It's remarkable how people will *quickly* open up to a good listener because they have seldom experienced that wonderful interaction and selfless experience. Who doesn't need and want to feel understood and appreciated? Your listening is actually a very therapeutic and healing activity for the person speaking.

Listening is often the only thing needed to help someone. It can not only be a sign of respect, but fondness or tenderness and affection as well. When a leader listens — really listens — regularly, his or her followers will become more loyal, dedicated and committed to the leader's goals because they feel both honored and respected to be listened to. William Shakespeare touched on listening's magnetic, "draw-them-to-me" quality, "When a lion fawns upon the lamb, the lamb will never cease to follow him."

Three: Gets Vital Information and Feelings. I discovered early in my career that often people hold back from telling you about things they think might come back to bite them or they may just downplay a problem (that might get worse), fearing that you, as manager, would punish or criticize them. Let's face it; it's a rare leader or manager who wants to hear what he or she doesn't want to hear. Empathic, non-judgmental and patient listening will open the floodgates of real information spewing out of your employees or others, that they would otherwise withhold from you. In addition, they will honestly and candidly share their feelings about things at work that affect their productivity, efficiency and quality of operations and performance.

My first assignment in Human Resources was as an employee relations manager. I found this to be the perfect entry point because in learning to do investigations, most of my job was to listen and gather all the information I could about the situation. I would then take it back to my leader, and she would help me apply HR practices.

As a leader, you can't fix or improve what you don't know about. With change and transformation in your organization, people might give the impression they support it, when in reality, they don't because they have fears and concerns about how changes will affect them. Your open-minded listening will uncover how people *really* feel, so you can adjust and improve your organizational transformation plans or strategies accordingly to accommodate them if you can. By frequently asking for their feedback, opinions and feelings, you can better quickly detect and solve problems and get their support for your change efforts. Knowledge is power because when asking well-thought-out, focused questions and listening completely, you will gain inside information that will be very useful to you. When you listen well, it's amazing what you can discover. When you act on what you've learned, it's amazing what you can change.

Four: Boosts Creativity and Innovation. One of the biggest complaints I've frequently heard about "management" is that they refuse to listen to fresh, new ideas, especially those original, bold and daring ones. Or if they do "entertain" new approaches, plans or solutions, for example, they do so to placate people, while not actively doing anything of value about them. After numerous times of management's not listening and following through, people become disengaged on the job, stop taking initiatives and go on "cruise control" — doing only the minimum of what's expected of them in their job definition. Opportunities are wasted! Morale and motivation are damaged. People leave to companies that want to hear about out-of-the-box ideas and non-conventional, potentially superior solutions.

Leaders and managers should always be approachable by inviting, encouraging and motivating people to come to them with any idea ranging from mild-to-wild. Even their audacious recommendations and proposed breakthrough solutions might be cleverly transformed into workable and practical ones that are far better than the mediocre ideas that are easy to come up with and implement. I remember reading it is easier to make powerful ideas practical than it is to make pedestrian ideas powerful.

In a March 2019 Fortune magazine article about the best companies to work for, it's mentioned that leaders directly influence how employees see the level of innovation in their company. The article highlights how employees with managers who are approachable and easy to talk with are *31 times* more likely to think their company is innovative. And when employees say that management genuinely seeks and responds to suggestions and ideas, they are *14 times* more likely to think their workplace is innovative and *4 times* more likely to think it's a great place to work. An organizational culture that encourages and promotes listening to any and all ideas is one where innovation flourishes and employees are more satisfied and proud to work there.

Five: Reduces Conflict and Promotes Reconciliation. All of us can relate to this situation. You and your spouse, partner or others close to you are arguing. Accusations and blame are flying back and forth. Emotions heat up, sometimes to a boiling point. Feelings are hurt. You feel he or she does not understand or is being "totally unreasonable." This back-and-forth bickering escalates in an unproductive waste-of-time. But at some point, you start listening and refrain from shouting or showing anger or frustration, but sincerely remain quiet and show him or her you care to understand where that person is coming from. Within a remarkably short period of time, the person realizes you do care and are not any longer being defensive and fighting back but want to fix the hurtful situation. Calm and reason slowly and gradually start coming forth, and heightened emotion starts fading. How long can someone argue and scream when the other person now is making a real, sincere attempt to comprehend and try to resolve the conflict by truly listening intently and openly.

At work, we all experience some degree and some frequency of conflict. Someone who seems unreasonable might vehemently disagree with a plan, strategy or proposed solution you are discussing at a meeting. They might be outright rude or nasty about how they disagree with you. Perhaps you did a great deal of research and analysis and arduously worked on it for a long time. You have a professional and emotional vested interest in it.

A person at the meeting known to be domineering and highly opinionated interrupts you before you finish describing your plan and solution jumps in and criticizes it in front of your peers. The natural inclination might be to immediately get defensive and then go on the offensive. If you can maintain self-control and calm, show lots of poise and quiet confidence and let the person go on while you listen politely without negative body language, your leadership image and credibility with your peers will be elevated, if not firmly established. Whether the person is trying to sabotage you or has genuine concerns (but is voicing them in unprofessional, emotional outbursts), your listening in an emotionally stable, secure and undisturbed way will handle that person magnificently and show your elevated bearing, stature and demeanor.

Six: Can Help with Persuasion and Influence. Today's and tomorrow's leaders are those who skillfully influence and persuade people to get greater cooperation, buy-in and commitment from them. Authoritarian leaders may still try to demand, tell, coerce or order compliance, but they won't get solid, eager collaboration that a soft approach will. Listening can help you influence, persuade and convince others. That sounds almost impractical until you realize the psychology behind it. Many salespeople, for instance, think that a compelling presentation and overt sales tactics get prospects to buy. What is the natural human tendency, however, when someone tries to sell us something without giving us an opportunity to warm up to the idea? They become guarded and defensive. The maxim is true, "people like to buy, but don't like to be sold."

Leaders can effectively sell their vision, plan, strategy or solution, for example, by warming followers up by listening to them after giving them a glimpse of those approaches. Call it "psychological reciprocity" in that when leaders, executives or managers show respect to their employees or followers by listening to their opinions, feedback or recommendations, then the employees will feel a sense of psychological obligation to listen openly in return, thus likely making them more receptive to what the leader is proposing. In that regard, listening carefully to someone when trying to influence, persuade, or convince them is a smart winning leadership strategy and behavior.

Overall, masterful listening will build better relationships and foster stronger trust with others, encourage people to give you more creative ideas, help reduce or resolve conflicts, provide you with lots of information that might have been kept secret or hidden before and help you influence others for support. Finally, by building up your listening muscle, you will be a more likable, respected and trusted leader.

Quick Listening Tips for Leaders

Here are brief listening techniques that I've found very useful in my growth as a leader and business executive throughout my career:

1. Get Ready. Every time you listen, especially in those very important interactions, get yourself mentally, physically and emotionally ready. Remind yourself to avoid distractions, concentrate and focus your full attention on the people speaking, and be aware of listening filters that would negatively affect your understanding and acceptance of messages, information and ideas. Put your phone away!

2. Show Positive Body Language. Use direct but comfortable eye contact with the speaker and have an open body position. For example, avoid crossing your arms across your chest, which might be perceived as being defensive or unaccepting of the message being given. Smile and nod your head (to show understanding or agreement), if called for. Lean forward toward the person when you want to show psychological support or extra interest in what is being said from an emotional standpoint. Avoid fidgeting, looking around or at your watch or seeming impatient.

3. Analyze and Evaluate What Is Being Said. While you are carefully listening, try to piece together the person's communication intentions, what his or her key messages are, what is *not* being said and what specific information the person is conveying that might be inaccurate or biased and what emotions are being expressed and why. Compare their viewpoint with yours. Finally, read the person's body language that will often unconsciously support or act against what they are saying.

4. Use "Verbal Encouragers." Silent ("deadpan") unresponsive listening can be quite uncomfortable to the person speaking. More natural listening involves timely interjecting of responses and phrases to let the person know you are fully listening and to keep the momentum of the discussion going forward. Examples of verbal encouragers are:

- ✓ Really - That's interesting
- ✓ You're absolutely right
- ✓ Makes sense to me
- ✓ Yes, please continue
- ✓ Isn't that true!
- ✓ I wonder why   - Hmm
- ✓ What happened then
- ✓ So, what did you think
- ✓ And   - Wow - Tell me more

5. Provide Effective Feedback and Paraphrasing. This active listening technique shows a listener's empathy, to confirm understanding of what is said and to sum up a speaker's message. With *feedback*, you repeat what someone says or ask to get confirmation. Example: "You want your team to get training on how to generate better ideas, and you want to give them more time during the week — at least 10 percent — to work on new ideas that might generate more business for your department." Sometimes a person speaking can be vague or ambiguous in their communication intent. A *paraphrase* can be used by you to try to state the essence of what someone is trying to say, though in their indirect or roundabout way. Example: "You're telling me that you've tried to support our transformation program, but your staff is finding it difficult to implement because of poor communication and direction from management. Is that really what you are saying?"

6. Reflection of Feelings. When you use this listening skill, it will not only show your understanding, sensitivity and appreciation for a person's feelings but will also help you as a leader better bond with that individual. If you're an executive, you can also better coach your managers using reflection of feelings. With this display of empathy, you attempt to put into words how you perceive that a person is feeling about something important to them. Examples: "With all the changes going on in our company, your job responsibilities can be very demanding, stressful and even very confusing." Or, "In our present culture, you can often feel unappreciated and unrewarded for all the hard work you and your group are doing." If you've accurately summed up their feelings, the person speaking will say something like, "That's how I feel!" or "You nailed that exactly right!"

7. Don't Interrupt or Show Impatience. This advice is critical, especially if people are emotional and trying to sincerely express their distressed feelings about something to you. When a listener frequently interrupts a speaker, it can annoy and frustrate that person and disrupt their flow of thought. However, sometimes verbose people can go on and on and on without getting to the point and only then you can interrupt to ask or say something like, "OK, the point you are making is precisely what?" or "Please briefly sum up what you want me to do about this situation?"

Being in a successful high-level executive or leadership position does not necessarily mean a person has refined listening skills. Numerous staff surveys show that managers, for example, regularly rate their listening proficiency skills higher than their employees do, so it's a good idea to work on being a better listener at all times. A valuable, general rule-of-thumb is to monitor your personal and professional conversations and try to keep somewhat of a 50/50 ratio of your talking-to-listening. Obviously, there are times at work when you might be doing 90 percent or more talking and only 10 percent or less listening and other situations call for you to ask questions perhaps or talk 20 percent of the time and listen to the answers or replies 80 percent of the time. Finally, realize one of the "downfalls" of being a good-to-great listener is that you will get some people to really open up… and talk and talk!

Transformative Leaders Ask Lots of Smart Questions

"Judge a man by his questions rather than his answers." – Voltaire

Along with active listening, leaders who are M.A.D. (Making A Difference) ask frequent and well-thought-out questions of people at all levels in their organization. You need the right information to make ideal decisions. I found that asking the right questions to the right people at the right times helps me to be a more informed and in-touch leader because it does several things:

One: It shows I genuinely care about people's ideas, opinions, feedback and their feelings.

Two: Questioning others gives me vital information firsthand rather than hearing it from others.

Three: It strengthens my rapport and relationships with my staff and helps reinforce trust between us.

Four: Asking questions and getting good answers can reduce misunderstandings and other miscommunications.

Five: Frequently questioning people in my organization improves my credibility and image as a transformation leader, who is out to make a difference for people and my organization.

Six: Asking roundabout questions can inspire more creativity and empower better solutions and ideas. Detailed questions will dig into a subject and guide and focus people's thinking toward fresh new perspectives and unique answers.

Seven: Questions enable me to properly and effectively coach my managers and employees to better performance.

In every organization, there are problems, frustrations, and underlying situations that impede effective performance. It could be politics, back-biting among groups, stifling rules and policies that are outdated and counterproductive, poor management or a negative culture or climate that stifles innovation or strategic transformation efforts. So, asking questions to dig deep into the symptoms and root causes of problems and getting to the real issues can be extremely beneficial. With active, empathic listening combined with good questioning techniques, a leader will not only allow, but encourage people to be (sometimes "brutally") candid with expressing their true feelings and offering unusual, bold ideas — even far-out ones — that might even turn out to be quantum leaps in results.

Use Open-Ended Questions

As a leader, you want to get people talking openly and fully expressing themselves. You do that with "open-ended questions" that begin with the words *what, why,* and *how.* Here are examples of these questions:

- *"What* is causing our teams to be more cautious and risk-averse with their ideas?"

- "In your opinion, *why* did this problem suddenly crop up?"

- *"How* do you think we should develop a good new marketing program given our limited budget?"

- Other ways to get more information from people along with their feelings include using phrases like these:

- *"Explain further* how your proposed solution would work with the current team we have in place."

- *"Tell me more* about feeling disappointed with how management is handling this new reorganization."

- *"I really want to know all about* how your innovative idea can give us a significant competitive edge over the next 2-3 years."

Valuable Questions That Managers and Leaders Should Ask

Famed management author and expert Peter Drucker recommended the five most important questions a leader will ask about his or her organization: What is our mission? Who is our customer? What does our customer value? What is our plan? What are our results? Here is an extremely useful, extensive list of questions for you to consider posing regularly to your managers, teams and individual employees. Getting effective answers from these questions could give you answers and ideas and solutions that will significantly alter the performance of your operations.

- "Is there a simpler (cheaper, better, quicker) solution or way of doing this?"

- "What should we stop doing?"

- What's most important to you and the team?"

- "What are you most proud of in your work?"

- "What are your current goals and plans?"

- "What opportunities should we be chasing and grabbing? What might prevent us from doing that, and what do we need to do?"

- "What concerns do you have? What frustrates you the most on the job?"

- "Describe and explain your proposed solution (idea, strategy, approach, roadmap, concept) to me."

- "What should we do to improve our processes?"

- "What market and technology trends should we keep a sharp eye on?"

- "How can we get our best ideas implemented faster and better?"

- "How can we manage resistance to our change (or transformation) program?"

- "What metrics should we use to measure innovation progress along with its risk?"

- "What barriers, obstacles, policies, red tape, politics or bureaucracy are hurting our efforts to be more innovative? What should be our priorities to reduce or eliminate them?"

- "Which one thing do you wish you've done differently on the job?"

- "How do we improve the value proposition our group offers to our company?"

- "What's the most important factor you consider when hiring someone?"

- "What's the biggest risk you've ever taken and what happened?"

- "How do you choose who to promote?"

- "What matters most to you in your job?"

- "If you were me, what would you do?"

- "What challenging (difficult, frustrating, painful) situation are you currently encountering? How is it impacting you, and what are you doing about it?"

- "How can you and your team (group, unit, department) be more creative and innovative on the job? What's holding you back?"

- "What do you need and want from management that you're not getting now?"

- "What does success look like?"

- "What's holding us back?"

- "How urgent or important is this?"

- "What will help us make better decisions?"

- "What are we neglecting to do that we should?"

- "Do you think our approach will be successful?"

- "How do you feel about that?"

- "What hasn't been achieved yet?"

- "How can we improve?"

- "What are people concerned about, but no one wants to say?"

- "Who best has experience with this?"

- "What's the answer in your opinion?"

- "What are your top priorities right now? How do you see them changing in the next 1-3 years from now? What are you doing about each priority and what has been your progress?"

- "What would you like to do, but feel you can't do it now because of....?"

- "How do we get people to show more initiative, to be more engaged and involved?"

- "What do I absolutely need to know about this issue (problem, opportunity, situation)?"

- "How can I best be of assistance to you?"

- "What is the current climate here, and why?"

- "Where do you want to go with this?"

- "What do you *think* about....? How do you *feel* about....?"

- "What is the best way we can make the most of this opportunity?"

Having a strategy to frequently ask the most meaningful questions to a smart and diverse group of people with different experiences, skills, knowledge and creative thinking will get you vital information to improve your organization and speed up innovation throughout it.

Omar's Bright Ideas

Summary for You to Make a Difference by Listening and Questioning

1. Make a goal to be a great listener. There are major benefits to becoming one!

2. Encourage all your staff to listen more. Be a role model for them.

3. Do not try to multitask and avoid distractions while listening to others. Give your full, undivided attention to the person speaking.

4. Review and practice the listening and questioning techniques in this chapter.

5. Encourage and openly listen to all types of creative ideas and recommendations for improvement from your employees.

6. Be on guard for listening filters you might have that will color and taint your listening.

7. Ask lots of meaningful questions (both "big picture" and detail-focused) to engage your staff and to find out valuable information to transform your organization.

8. Be very aware not to frequently interrupt others while they are speaking.

9. While you are listening, think like a detective trying to figure out and find clues to what people are *really* saying and meaning.

10. Remember, listening is a tough, sometimes draining activity, but it's worthwhile for a leader.

Chapter 6

Give W-O-W! Speeches and Presentations
Captivate, Excite and Compel Your Audiences to Take Action

"Speech is power: speech is to persuade, to convert, to compel."
– Ralph Waldo Emerson

Great leaders throughout the ages have been consummate communicators and dynamic public speakers. They inspired and galvanizd the masses of people to their causes and mission. I'm not shocking you to tell you that too many managers, executives and people in leadership positions today are mediocre public speakers and business presenters. You already know that. I admit that I needed improvement in my business presentations and public speeches as most of us do, and what a difference it made for me when I worked at it! I became a strong speaker, and it benefitted my overall leadership activities. Today, I continue to perfect and hone my speaking.

If you are going to make a difference in your job and life, you must move people emotionally and intellectually while you're speaking. In this detailed and comprehensive chapter, I'll share with you about some leaders catapulted into fame primarily because of their speaking abilities. And I'll tell you why they were powerful speakers. Finally, I'll leave you with some valuable tips and techniques that I've found incredibly useful. As a result, you can be a more impressive and admired executive and leader who can get better results faster.

Many business presenters think it's all about the content of one's speech or presentation. While valuable information is obviously very important, always remember that YOU are the message. Everything you say and do causes people to make judgments about your messages, what you stand for, and what kind of leader you are. If they don't buy into *you,* they won't with your ideas, proposals or plans.

The terms "speech" and "presentation" are often used interchangeably. A speech is typically more formal and seldom uses visuals. A presentation almost always uses visuals to inform, educate, sell something or get buy-in to an idea, solution, proposal or plan and strategy, for example. Strong leaders are skilled in delivering both speeches and business presentations.

Have you experienced something like the following before? As the opening speaker, the big boss gets up in front of hundreds of people at one of your company's big events. He gets to the lectern, fiddles with his notes, moves the microphone and has a momentary bit of delay getting his computer to play his PowerPoint deck. He coughs, lowers his head and buries his eyes in his notes and reads them word-for-word, just as he does on his text-filled slides. Holding onto the podium as if his hands were superglued to the sides, his eyes darting back and forth between his notes and the screen and with his monotone delivery, 10 minutes later into his 30-minute talk, you see people in the middle and back of the room sneaking peeks into their phones while others are forcing themselves not to yawn as their eyelids start to droop.

No one will remember what he had to say (because nothing really stood out) unless they knew they had to take a test afterward and I suspect many just might not pass. As for his conclusion, he ended with "Well, I guess that's about all I have to say." Polite applause and a feeling of deep relief followed. His attitude was, "I don't have to be a great speaker. I'm good already. Besides, I'm the boss. They HAVE TO listen to me!"

The CEO was followed by the Executive Vice President of Sales and Marketing. After being introduced, she energetically walked to the lectern, all the while smiling and looking at the audience. Her interesting and imaginative introduction immediately grabbed the group's attention. Within a minute, she walked away from the lectern and moved around on stage, articulately speaking without notes and using a remote to change the slides in her presentation, which, instead of having a lot of text, had meaningful photos, attractive charts, creative illustrations and two brief, gripping videos.

She did a wonderful job using humor, anecdotes, examples, and analogies, along with her three fascinating short stories that captivated the group while giving them relevant information that people remembered and talked about weeks later. Her confident voice and poised, yet powerful body language reinforced her messages. Her presentation conclusion was so well-prepared, clever and psychologically compelling, that it, along with her overall creative presentation, had a motivational and intellectual impact on people. What a world of difference between those two speakers and what a difference she made with those in the audience.

Being a Great Speaker Can Brightly Spotlight You as a Strong Leader

What can you tell about a person after seeing him or her for your first time give a speech or business presentation? Actually, you can discover (or at least perceive) more about people than just about any other activity or behaviors they participate in. Giving a speech or presentation is an all-inclusive showcase for the "totality" of a person. Here are some things you might likely discern about speakers/presenters or at least make assumptions about how they come across based upon *what* they say and *how* they say it along with their voice qualities, body language, personality and appearance:

• education level
• emotional intelligence
• trustworthiness
• experience
• competence
• leadership ability
• tactfulness
• sense of humor
• character

- social skills
- motives
- economic status
- confidence
- people skills
- sophistication
- stage presence
- charisma
- values
- professionalism
- decisiveness
- innovative
- open-minded
- visionary
- optimism
- risk-taking
- organized
- engaging
- beliefs

It's a proven fact that being a polished and dynamic speaker and business presenter will boost one's leadership aura and create a sterling impression of a person sometimes beyond the reality of who he or she really is. Lowell Thomas, the famous writer, actor and radio broadcaster from decades ago, put that into clear perspective, "The ability to speak is a shortcut to distinction. It puts a man in the limelight, raises him head and shoulders above the crowd, and the man who can speak acceptably is usually given credit for an ability out of proportion to what he really possesses."

Unfortunately, a very competent, smart, ethical and dedicated individual with below-par public speaking and communication skills, appearance and presence can have less credibility and professional impact. It may seem superficial, shallow and unfair, but great ideas, potential solutions and plans have fallen victim to the weaknesses of the person presenting them.

What Do Executives and Leaders Want from People Presenting to Them?

A comprehensive survey of senior executives was performed by GenesisTraining Solutions and highlighted in several books. It consisted of 20 multiple-choice questions and 5 open-ended questions. Some of the results were quite surprising, while others confirmed what presentation experts tell us and the rest of us feel and experience. Here are a few of the key findings:

- Executives were asked to rate the overall quality of presentations given to them. They said 38 percent of the presentations they typically attend were "acceptable" in quality, 23 percent of those presentations were considered "mediocre" and only 8 percent were considered excellent. That means there is a wide-open opportunity for a presenter to make a substantial positive impression and help their career by giving an outstanding presentation to high-level decision-makers.

- What impressed executives about presenters was for them to be absolute masters of the information they were giving. This was key for their credibility. As Clarence B. Randall, lawyer, businessman and advisor to two U.S. Presidents, said, "The leader must know, must know that he knows, and must be able to make it abundantly clear to those around him that he knows."

- They believe a strong and clear presentation introduction and conclusion are critical.

- Executives felt the overall quality of visuals used by presenters should be much better in terms of giving information that is clear, concise and convincing.

- In presentation "style," those surveyed said they preferred speakers who are informal, relaxed and conversational in their presenting style as opposed to either formal and conservative or consistently high energy/lively/enthusiastic styles like motivational speakers. Showing sincere passion is good if it's not overdone or exaggerated. Younger executives and leaders like higher energy from speakers, while older, more conservative ones prefer genuine enthusiasm, but toned down a bit.

- The "deadly sins" as you might have imagined are presenters who display a lack of integrity, such as faking an answer, misrepresenting facts, unreasonably exaggerating, being indiscreet, acting pompous or arrogant, being ill-prepared or unsure of their subject knowledge.

Texan Edward (Ed) Whitacre, Jr. was a former chairman of the board and Chief Executive Officer (CEO) of AT&T Inc. He took the position as chairman and interim CEO of General Motors (GM) when it emerged from bankruptcy in July 2009. In his book, *American Turnaround: Reinventing AT&T and GM and the Way We Do Business in the USA,* he talked about the poor state of presentations at GM, where executives who presented to him always had complex PowerPoint presentations with a large number of slides that were overflowing with small text and comprehensive charts.

Whitacre was frustrated and annoyed listening to these "PowerPoint Rangers" with their inflexible, inefficient and restrictive ways of communicating. He said, "If someone came in to see me and started in with those (PowerPoint) slides, I'd say, 'Wait, stop' and make them shut it down and talk to me. I don't need all those charts. I just need to know the end conclusion or larger point — tell me that, and then let's talk about it. But tell me — don't point with some laser from the other end of the room and click, click through fifty slides…"

Whitacre coached these presenters before board meetings and recommended they prepare brief — ten minutes maximum — presentations that eliminated wordy explanations, lots of financial and operational details and, instead, just focus on need-to-know information — things that related directly to GM's business and the bottom line. This pleased the board members who instead of sitting through mind-numbing daylong meetings, could now ask questions and become more engaged through this new concise and interactive presentation format.

Accomplished Speakers Inspire, Motivate and Move Us

Public speaking is the most common and visible characteristic of leadership. Everyone who speaks publicly can potentially be seen as a leader. Politicians get elected because of it, entrepreneurs get massive funding because they present so well, military leaders get their plans and strategies approved because they are credible and convincing presenters, and businesspeople race up their career ladder after giving ultra-impressive presentations, TV interviews and speeches that spotlight and showcase their abilities and companies. The important speeches of leaders are a call to action, not to discuss, analyze, ponder or hesitate. "Follow me, and you will benefit and be part of something bigger and better" is their message.

In the third most viewed Ted talk of all time — by over 47 million people — Simon Sinek tells how great leaders inspire action. They start with "Why." I encourage you to watch and learn from his call to action.

It's often amazing to see how highly successful motivational speakers like veteran Les Brown can easily hold his audience right in the palm of his hand every speech he makes or how Tony Robbins can whip thousands of people into an energetic and emotional frenzy. It's powerful, it's magical and it can be scary with the wrong person (a self-serving narcissist, sociopath or dictator) gaining those commanding and seemingly mystical speaking skills.

Their Speaking Mastery Catapulted Them to World Leadership

Crises do not create heroes and great leaders… they simply reveal them. And this is perfectly illustrated during World War II with Winston Churchill, Franklin D. Roosevelt, Benito Mussolini, Adolf Hitler and Joseph Stalin. Being powerful, charismatic speakers (except for Stalin) played a major role in their rise to power and their ability to galvanize and move the masses to reach their objectives. Obviously, Hitler and Mussolini were on the evil, dark side of history, but were it not for their stirring, electrified speeches, they would likely be small blots in the fabric of those times.

President Franklin D. Roosevelt, while not a stereotypical charismatic speaker (although a charming, polished and effective one), knew how to uplift and calm Americans, give them hope and faith to persevere during the Depression, and he instilled confidence in them and the will to win the ravaging war in Europe and the Pacific. His warm, personal "fireside chats with his down-home way of talking" comforted people, and they respected, loved and trusted him as a result. He could be wonderfully informal or formal (with great presence) in his speaking styles.

Winston Churchill was called the "British Bulldog" perhaps because of his sturdy, short stature, tough tenaciousness, "dogged determination" and the fact that many said he resembled his bulldog named Dodo. He was a charismatic leader and speaker and Prime Minister of Britain when Britain needed him the most. The Nazis, in their lightening blitzkrieg across Europe during 1940 quickly defeated a number of countries including France in June of that year. Most people might not know that after this rout, the leaders in Britain were close to signing a treaty with Hitler to avoid a bloodbath, were it not for Churchill who, through his courageous leadership and persuasion convinced them to fight.

Not only a superb, strong and persevering wartime leader, Churchill was also a charismatic speaker who inspired his people, gave them the firmness and resolve to fight and cheered them on relentlessly during the darkest days of the Second World War. Through his speeches and appearances, he steeled the population to withstand the onslaught of bombers in their cities and emboldened his soldiers, sailors and airmen to win the battles they fought around the world.

6. GIVE W-O-W! SPEECHES AND PRESENTATIONS

Besides his firm leadership, Churchill's stirring oratory is part of his greatest and enduring legacy. Few speakers throughout history matched his skill in using advanced speech techniques to impact his listeners. In a lot of respects, Churchill was focused on performing, not just delivering a speech. He became a master of what today we call memorable soundbites such as "This was their finest hour," and "Never in the field of human conflict was so much owed by so many to so few" and "I have nothing to offer but blood, toil, tears and sweat."

A Magnificent Speaker and Leader Who Changed the Course of American History

Researchers at the University of Wisconsin-Madison and Texas A&M University compiled a list of 100 best political speeches of the 20th century — words that shook the world and reminded us of the enormous power of public speaking. This list comprised the opinions of 137 scholars of American public address. These experts were asked to evaluate and recommend speeches based upon their excellence of oratory, bold statements, rhetorical artistry and widespread social and political impact and ultimate results.

At the top of their list was Dr. Martin Luther King Jr.s' famous "I Have A Dream," often considered a perfect, flawless speech. On the Mall in Washington D.C. during the "March On Washington," on August 28, 1963, Dr. King held spellbound about 250,000 people at the event and millions on television and did what mere mortal speakers could not. Others in the top 10 of the best political speeches were JFK, Richard Nixon, Ronald Reagan and Lyndon Johnson. Three of the top 10 speeches were delivered by African Americans (including Barbara Jordan and Malcolm X), and twenty-three of the top 100 were given by women).

People were profoundly touched in their souls and electrified by such an elegant, poetic and emotional speech delivered by an eloquent master speaker at a momentous time in history. All that came together for a historic defining moment, never likely to be repeated like that again. A dignified Dr. King spoke with such stirring, sincere emotion that naturally sprang forth from his genuinely intense belief in his message and virtuous cause.

"I have a Dream" speech contained 1,667 words and took him only 17 minutes to deliver it. It was clear, concise, convincing, captivating and compelling. Like all superb principled speeches, Dr King drew his references from a wide variety of sources, including the Bible, Gettysburg Address, the Emancipation Proclamation, the US Declaration of Independence, the Constitution and Shakespeare. His richly constructed content and language used contrasts, metaphors, vivid language, repetition, and emphasis, all delivered in superb cadence and vocal variation that dug into the listener's head and heart like a jackhammer.

His call to action was clear, decisive and irresistible, and he brilliantly ended on a high note. Instead of expressing seething anger, negativism or calling for even a hint violent or aggressive resistance, he filled his words with psychological reason, optimism and a positive sense and hope that righteousness and justice, as written by the American founding fathers, will prevail.

In many respects, the speech was creative and had not a scintilla of boring content in that it avoided common language, dry facts and jargon, and instead used imaginative communication tools such as memorable and poignant metaphors that evoked emotions, common threads and colorful imagery. He painted a vivid picture of the plight of African-Americans, "living on a lonely island in the midst of a vast ocean of material poverty." Perhaps his most splendid and praiseworthy metaphor with its evocative language was this one:

"In a sense, we've come to our nation's capital to cash a check. When the architects of our republic wrote the magnificent words of the Constitution and the Declaration of Independence, they were signing a promissory note to which every American was to fall heir. Instead of honoring this sacred obligation, America has given the Negro people a bad check, a check that has come back marked 'insufficient funds.' But we refuse to believe that the bank of justice is bankrupt. We refuse to believe that there are insufficient funds in the great vaults of opportunity of this nation. And, so we've come to cash this check, a check that will give us upon demand the riches of freedom and the security of justice."

Dr. King was a master of using repetition of his theme or key phase to imbed his main point throughout his talk. Again and again at strategic points inns speech, he would pause and repeat "I have a Dream" to enable the audience to fixate on it — the essence of his message.

Whether it is a public speech, or a business presentation, you're being creative with catchy, deeply meaningful and attention-riveting contrasts/comparisons, metaphors, stories, examples and other communication tools will enable people not just to hear, but see, feel and "experience" the words and visuals you deliver for them. As a speaker, strive to perform something different and better than the crowd. Do what novelist James Michener advised, "taking ordinary words and doing something extraordinary with them" as Dr. King's speech perfectly exemplified.

Like all great speakers, Dr. King prepared and practiced his speech so he could deliver most of it without notes. As a leader myself, I learned that practice of speaking skills is critical and then I rehearse and rehearse the content of each new presentation I will give until it flows naturally and easily without my using notes or even slides sometimes.

As a result of his speech, Dr King was named Man of the Year by Time Magazine in 1963 and won the Nobel Peace Prize the following year. That's the leadership power of being an accomplished and moving speaker! Very few of us can speak anywhere near the power, authority and impact that Dr. King did. Because he set such a high bar, that doesn't mean any of us should not raise our own bar of working toward being as good of a public speaker and presenter as we can. Howard Gardner, in his book *Leading Minds*, tells the reader that all successful leaders have essentially two things in common — an overarching story and a life that embodies and showcases that story. What's your story, and how are you living it and telling it?

Becoming a Captivating and Compelling Speaker

I can't emphasize enough the importance, impact and power of a leader being a great communicator, public speaker and business presenter. Becoming better at those has enriched my own professional image and boosted my ability to engage people better and lead them. Two of my favorite words relating to this topic are "captivating" and "compelling." When you *captivate* a group with your speaking skills, you grab and "super-glue" hold the attention and full interest of a group or large audience. They are delighted, fascinated, intrigued and enthralled by you and how you own and command the stage or meeting room.

Your voice, body language, creativity, charisma and personality play a huge role in riveting their interest. A captivating speaker is dynamic, confident, expressive, energetic, passionate, perhaps entertaining, humorous and enjoyable — even fun — to watch and listen to. The best platform speakers know how to create curiosity, focus your attention, and even add a sense of theatrical excitement to a presentation. While these consummate speakers are professional in every sense, they also consider themselves "performers" as well.

A *compelling* speaker makes their proposal, solution, idea or strategy seem absolutely irresistible (a synonym for compelling). They methodically take information and shape it in ways that appeal to a group's logic, rationale, needs, wants, emotions and aspirations. At the end of a compelling speech or presentation, the audience will not just give a standing ovation or vigorous applause or express deep admiration, they are motivated, energized and galvanized to action — to do what the speaker wants them to do.

How you use critical information, organize it, prioritize it and precisely target it at an audience's needs and wants plays a key role in making your presentation compelling. Information is *giving out,* but communication is *getting through,* and if you get through as a result, they are likely convinced, persuaded and ready to support and commit to what you recommend. With being captivating and compelling, you and your speech or presentation will be remembered long after they leave. And your career will get a shot of powerful adrenalin. If you want to be a game-changer, a disruptor and an innovator, then transforming yourself into a better speaker and presenter will work wonders. One way to do that is to be an exemplary storyteller.

Storytelling — A Leader's "Must Have" Skill

When you tell some business executives to develop applicable "stories" for their presentations or speeches, many give you a puzzled look as if to say, "What's wrong with hard-core facts and statistics?" Yet Richard Branson, Elon Musk, Steve Jobs, (and especially) Walt Disney along with U.S. Presidents use moving stories that happen to include facts, statistics, examples, analogies and other communication elements. Motivational speakers like Tony Robbins and actor Denzel Washington (who is a powerful inspirational speaker, not just great actor) often share stories, that are unforgettable, the centerpiece of their topics. The best TED Talks have stories as their "magic ingredient."

Storytellers can not only inspire and motivate us, but they can also teach us, persuade us, ignite movements, and help us to open our minds to more of the possibilities and opportunities that life has to offer. Roger Schank, an artificial intelligence theorist, remarked, "Humans are not ideally set up to understand logic; they are ideally set up to understand stories." Having a good story can showcase your brand, explain your organization's impressive history, provide the listener with a better understanding of your values, and help you to grow and prosper your business.

When I was invited to Bloomberg's Washington DC office on K-Street to participate in a nationally broadcast event on organizational shared services transformation by Phil Searle of Chazzey Partners, I knew the story was going to be more important than the statistics. During the 30 minutes, I tried to paint a picture of our transformative journey through words. I talked about the lack of technology and had visuals to prove my points. I remember saying we started off with typewriter and carbon paper and moved to automated workflows.

A good story is the only way to activate parts in our brain so we turn that story into our own idea and experience. Research tells us that messages delivered as stories can be over 20 times more memorable than just facts. Search the web for articles on how to tell stories for your presentations and buy some books about it and then practice and hone your stories so they will significantly help your speeches and make you a better leader and communicator.

Comprehensive Checklist of Quick Tips and Reminders

Here is a full list of valuable tips, techniques and recommendations I've learned and fine-tuned that have helped me to be a significantly better speaker, presenter and communicator I want to share with you:

✓ Understand your audience, what they want and need from your speech or presentation. Find out what they already know about your topic and customize it for them. No one shows up at a financial conference to talk about fishing.

✓ Whether you use PowerPoint or some other presentation app like Apple's Keynote, make your visuals simple, attractive, easy to read and limit the text on them. Use relevant photos, illustrations, graphics, charts, animations (for example, using Adobe After Effects) and videos all designed to better explain, describe and justify your main points than primarily words and numbers. Have your visuals show interconnections, relationships, cause-and effects and trends, instead of just isolated facts or statistics. Answer, "What does it mean?" Avoid being a "PowerPoint Ranger" who dumps text on every slide and reads it word-for-word!

✓ Determine your presentation or speech objectives — what do you actually want from your audience? What do you want them to know, to believe, to feel, to be convinced of, to agree with you, to support you, or to approve your request? What do you need them to act upon after your presentation?

✓ Keep your enthusiasm, energy and passion high enough for each group. Younger people love a "pumped-up" presenter, while older or more conservative audiences prefer a more toned-down, but still lively speaker.

✓ Develop and make a riveting, attention-grabbing introduction and a powerful, memorable conclusion. Spend a disproportionate percentage of time crafting these because of their importance.

✓ Keep it simple and your focus only on the 2-3 priorities or key messages of your speech that will enable you to reach your objectives. Use only enough information so your group will easily understand, agree with you, make a decision you want them to, or somehow act upon your request or recommendation. Richard Branson once said, "If your pitch can't fit on the back of an envelope, it's rubbish."

✓ Develop quick, strong rapport with your audiences and earn their trust and respect.

✓ Radiate a professional, confident and in-charge "Command Presence Leadership" aura and stance without appearing overbearing, aggressive or authoritative.

✓ Be flexible and dynamically adapt and modify the presentation to meet changing audience needs, requests and preferences.

✓ Make your speech or presentation (even mildly) entertaining if possible, or at least highly interesting and enjoyable. Late night talk show host Johnny Carson rightfully said, "People will pay more to be entertained than informed."

✓ Make your key presentation points and messages "snap, crackle and pop!" by emphasizing and highlighting them, so they clearly stand out.

✓ Whether subtly or directly, pull the heartstrings of people in your audiences to impact them emotionally as well as intellectually to motivate, uplift, encourage, compliment, inspire and, if necessary, galvanize them to action.

✓ Take complex and difficult-to-understand topics and strive to "elegantly simplify" them for ease of understanding and decision-making.

✓ Display effective body language (posture, movement, gestures, eye contact, facial expressions) and vocal techniques (volume, rate, inflection, pauses) to rivet the attention of people.

✓ Smartly use various ways to repeat key messages and critical information to make it stick in the minds and hearts of people.

✓ Tell great stories that supplement the other information you provide.

✓ Apply presentation technology (hardware, software and apps) in smart ways to showcase and amplify your communication points.

✓ Speak with authority and but in a warm, natural, sincere and conversational way.

✓ Ensure your appearance —grooming, hair, dress, accessories — is tasteful, top-notch and appropriate to the occasion. And conduct yourself like the quintessential professional.

✓ Display masterful knowledge of the topics of the speech or presentation.

✓ Show competence in answering questions and dealing with comments from the audience. Be "cool-under-fire" if someone confronts or challenges you.

✓ Carefully watch and listen to the audience to detect clues on how people are reacting to your presentation and then appropriately respond to meet your objectives.

6. GIVE W-O-W! SPEECHES AND PRESENTATIONS

✓ Engage and interact with the audience and even "play with them" (when appropriate) to get their participation and lock in their attention.

✓ Don't just speak well, but "perform" professionally. Have fun on stage. Show that you're not only comfortable but also enjoying it.

✓ Try not to get ruffled by hostile or aggressive audience members. Don't get unhinged or defensive (even by an obnoxious "heckler"). Instead, act controlled and cool under fire." Be prepared for any resistance, objections or negative behavior during a potentially controversial topic or proposal you give.

Strategies for Becoming a Better Speaker

Here are a few effective ways to develop or just fine-tune your speaking abilities that will enhance your leadership results:

- Get a good, experienced speech coach who will videotape your presentations, then give you detailed feedback on your content, vocal delivery and body language and also tips on your PowerPoint or Keynote visuals.

- Practice, practice, practice. Remember famous football coach Vince Lombardi who advised, "Practice does not make perfect. Only perfect practice makes perfect."

- Go on YouTube and look at videos of motivational speakers, popular keynote and TED speakers. Observe and listen to how they command their audiences. Learn from them, but don't copy their style. Be you, but be the "best you."

- Consider joining Toastmasters International, where you can give a brief talk and get feedback at the meetings.

- Buy books on speaking and presenting.

Omar's Bright Ideas

Summary for You to Make a Difference by Being a More Riveting Speaker

1. Being a better public speaker and business presenter will do wonders for your leadership career.

2. Don't give typical, PowerPoint presentations filled with text. Get creative with your visuals and videos. Keep it simple, but relevant and interesting.

3. Review my chapters on charisma and presence and incorporate those ideas and behaviors in your speeches.

4. Develop and combine poise, polish, power and persuasion in ways that make you stand out and above other leaders and speakers.

5. Study how the "speaking masters" captivate audiences. Go online and see videos of speakers from the past and present. Watch and listen to see what you can learn from them. A great book to read is *Speeches That Changed The World* by Quercus Publishing.

6. Videotape your (live and practiced) speeches and presentations to see what you need to change and also consider getting a speech coach to significantly improve.

7. When the situation calls for it, add humor, props, fascinating visuals and videos and other and other elements of showmanship. Even if you tone it down, you'll come across more interesting than more "buttoned down, plain vanilla" presenters.

8. Don't read your slides word-for-word. Try to memorize limited, but important information — key points, vital statistics, quotations and other priority information — so you can talk more conversationally and informally with your groups.

9. Read your audience for clues on how the message is being received. Change your approach if you are losing their interest. Be adaptable.

10. Learn and become proficient in the art of great storytelling — stories that create curiosity, anticipation and even intrigue, yet can contain relevant facts, statistics, metaphors, comparisons/contrasts "aha moments" and other elements of public speaking.

Become a master of your topic. That will ensure your credibility, make it easy to answer even tough questions and ease your stage fright if you have any.

Chapter 7

Powering Up Your Leadership "X Factor"
Adding Extra Charisma to Your Style

"Charisma is a sparkle in people that money can't buy. It's an invisible energy with visible effects."
– Marianne Williamson

Charismatic leaders are exciting to be around and work with. This extraordinary form of emotion-laden, symbolic and values-based leadership can be ideal at stimulating and encouraging certain critical behaviors and motivating followers by way of eloquent and persuasive communication and force of personality. These transformational leaders can energize, stimulate, motivate and galvanize people to reach tough and taxing and sometimes "impossible" goals and visions. They can be invaluable in organizations where this uncanny charismatic ability to influence people can bring about great change and innovation when desperately needed.

Barbara Corcoran, who is one of the talented investors on the popular television show *Shark Tank* emphasized, "I don't invest in entrepreneurs anymore who don't have charisma." If you want your organization to be more entrepreneurial and innovative, you will benefit from select leaders who have a super potent personal and professional mix of charisma, character and competency. Then, stand back and watch them work wonders.

To be inspired is great. To inspire others is incredible, and that's what a charismatic executive or leader can do like no other. That means the right charismatic leader can embolden and empower individuals, teams and entire departments to come up with mind-warping creative ideas while pushing and supporting them to implement those big ideas effectively. Charismatic leaders can communicate with people they lead on an emotional level, being masters at tapping into their pride, aspirations, hopes, needs and wants. They almost always possess superb (some have transcendent) oratorical skills. That can work for the good or bad of organizations and society as we'll see later.

Adding charisma — also called the "IT" or "X" Factor — to one's leadership inventory (yes, you can learn to be more charismatic as you'll discover) will help drive any organization toward a worthwhile, compelling vision in times of opportunity, to win victory in times of war or conflict or garner success in times of disaster or upheaval. Such leaders appeared whenever there was a need to quickly unite and mobilize the masses and get them to dedicate and perform at higher levels for some common cause or to best deal with traumatic change. Think Alexander the Great, FDR, Winston Churchill, Nelson Mandela, Steve Jobs, and Martin Luther King Jr., among many others.

Down-to-earth actor George Clooney makes being witty, charming and humorous an effortless affair and his sparkling personality and elegant ease of delightful conversation warmly engage people in real life as well. Oprah stands out as one of the best in the entertainment business at exhibiting a sophisticated, but somewhat toned-down and polished, but still impacting the type of charisma that magnetically draws people to her. Her ability to engage people to open up and feel comfortable and special is legendary.

Is having charisma always necessary for your successful leadership or management? No. Business leader and author Douglas Conant said, "Most people think of leaders as being these outgoing, very visible, and charismatic people, which I find to be a very narrow perception. You might just find that you have introverts embedded within your organization who are natural-born leaders." I generally agree, but, certain forms of charisma, when added to other ingredients in your recipe for leadership effectiveness, can make a real difference in how you lead and the results you get. In this chapter, I'll explain what this exceptional quality is, what impact it has on others, and most importantly, how you can strengthen your charisma muscle if you wish.

7. POWERING UP YOUR LEADERSHIP "X FACTOR"

It's been said that the ideal way for leaders or executives to get followers and employees committed to them and their vision, mission and ideas is to get people to 1. like; 2. Respect; and 3. trust them. That's the ultimate "bonding trilogy!" Did you ever notice how some people brightly stand out and above the crowd? When they walk into a room or social setting, all heads turn to notice and observe. It might amaze you that after shaking their hands, making eye contact with them and "B-O-O-M!" — you instantly like, and somehow trust and believe them? It's an attractiveness and appeal that gives beyond one's good looks or overall appearance.

By developing and strengthening your charisma qualities:

- You will seem powerful and dynamic without being intimidating.

- People will admire you, want to be around you and feel energized by you.

- You will exude confidence, be at ease and comfortable with yourself.

- Expect to get more attention and respect from most people.

- You'll be enjoyable and perhaps even fun to be with.

- It will easier to persuade others and get what you want because people will be more inclined to help you.

Charisma is called the "X Factor" For a Good Reason: It's Magnetic

A woman who attended a recent rally for a political candidate said of him, "He has it. Whatever IT is, he has it." Various politicians, entertainers, motivational speakers, high-powered clergy, military leaders and business executives are often pictured possessing charisma, but your local auto mechanic, high school coach, retail store clerk, stay-at-home mom or anyone can be fortunate enough to have this sparkling personality gift.

Charisma, like presence (in a following chapter) has a mysterious and elusive quality to it. We know right away that someone has this dynamic trait that attracts and pulls people to them and can inspire devotion from others, but we're stymied to try to precisely describe it because there are numerous charismatic people with different mixes of personalities, characters and styles. Someone metaphorically described charisma as "smiling out loud!" A 2017 University of Toronto study found that observers watching a silent recording of a person delivering a speech will decide whether a person is charismatic in as little as five seconds!

The English term *charisma* is derived from the Greek *khárisma*, which meant "gift of grace" or "favor freely given." The ancient Greeks attributed personality charisma characteristics such as beauty, creativity and charm to their gods. Today, some synonyms and terms used to describe charisma are alluring, joie de vivre, bewitching, captivating, glamorous, appealing, dazzling, exuberance, positive energy, fascinating, enchanting, charming, flashy, animal magnetism, having pizzazz, star quality or drawing power, being irresistible, attractive and having sex appeal. No doubt that possessing and using aspects of these for positive results will add to one's image and success.

One thing though that stands out about all charismatic people is that they project confidence, not in an arrogant or puffed-up way, but in a composed, assured and genuine fashion. Gabourey Sidibe, who made her acting debut in the film *Precious* and was nominated for the Academy Award for best actress, said that people always asked her, "You have so much confidence. Where did that come from?" She would say, "It came from me. One day I decided I was beautiful, and so I carried my life as if I were a beautiful girl."

Each of us might uniquely judge a person to be charismatic. Someone can be charismatic to me, but not to you. There are degrees of charisma that people possess. Some with an intense abundance of it can project charisma like a high voltage sizzling bolt of lightning zapping us, while others have a comfortable, pleasant, more subtle charisma that makes us feel like a pair of comfortable emotional slippers enveloping us. You would likely agree that Will Smith, Bill Clinton, Denzel Washington, Muhammad Ali, Sofia Vergara exude charisma right out of their pores. Late comedian Robin Williams was surely a human dynamo of non-stop "electrified charisma" and brilliant talent.

High energy and flashy exuberance doesn't describe the likes, for example, of U.S. Presidents John F. Kennedy (JFK), Franklin D. Roosevelt (FDR) and Ronald Reagan who are characteristically viewed as having a form of understated, but still solid charisma that affected people around the world. President Barack Obama was known as an introvert, contrary to how so many people perceived him publicly, yet he exhibited a wide range of polished charisma and adapted his personality to be extraverted and outgoing when needed. These former presidents had smiles, warmth, repartee, humor, charm and excellent speech and communication skills that cemented their place in history as being, in fact, charismatic leaders and people. And, of course, their noble bearing amplified their image of being charismatic.

For leaders, it definitely helps to be charismatic, especially when companies, organizations and countries are experiencing great competition, challenges, threats, and even dangers. That's because charisma emotionally engages and uplifts followers and inspires and motivates them to a cause or specific action, somewhat similar to how charismatic actors tap into the deep emotional reveries of moviegoers in their story.

On-Demand Charisma When Needed

Many celebrities, leaders, sports figures and executives, for example, can come across magnificently charismatic "on demand" — at meetings, when public speaking on stage to large groups or in a sports arena, while being much less so charismatic in private. They can be introverted and even shy, when not "on." They're able to impressively light up and energize when performing, then revert to their more staid personalities when not in the spotlight.

As a speaker, I know when the stage lights go on it's my time to shine. A few summers ago, I had an intern following me around our organization. Earlier that morning I have been asked to speak to a group of leaders on innovation. The invitation was last minute and the young man asked me if I knew what I was going to say. My answer was absolutely not. However, by the time I stepped up to the lectern, I had formulated a plan and delivered what was an inspiring and motivating talk on innovation. If you know your information and key messages, you are always "ready."

Somehow it is easier to be charismatic when playing a role in business or a character in a movie or assuming a different persona as an entertainer. In these situations, people "permit" themselves to be different — assertive, charming, beguiling, courageous, outspoken, funny, romantic, daring or dangerous than they would ordinarily behave. They can take risks and become someone they normally would not be because their role or character demands it. When the director yells, "Cut... Print It!" they revert to being themselves like the rest of us until the next scene requires their character to "light up." They have "contextual charisma" and so can you as a manager, executive or military, community or government leader.

Bet you didn't know that famous singer, songwriter, and musician Prince, whose career spanned four decades, almost didn't become famous. How is that possible since he is known for his incredible artistry, talent, creativity and flamboyant stage presence? Well, representatives from Warner Records first saw him at a showcase performance in a small Minneapolis theatre in January 1979 and thought he was an excellent musician but was not ready for a tour. They felt he wasn't a good enough "performer" — that he seemed awkward on stage, that he lacked charisma and did not know how to engage and excite the crowd.

A fortunate break came for Prince when singer Rick James of "Super Freak" fame asked Prince to open up one of his tours in 1980. At the time, James said, "I felt sorry for him." But James later saw that Prince was dead set on improving. Prince adopted the performance tactics and stage confidence of performers he admired (including that of James) and improve, he certainly did. Prince believed that charisma and stage presence could be learned, practiced and perfected — and he was right. The results obviously were spectacular for him!

Another surprise is the super-creative and talented Lady Gaga, who, like so many other world-renowned artists and celebrities, can wonderfully assume a commanding, magnificently self-assured stage persona, and yet be more of a shrinking violet in everyday life, as she opens up with, "I might not be shy with people that I know, but with people that I don't know, I am very shy ... I always feel shy in the Hollywood scene. I feel a bit like I did in high school, like I don't really fit in."

The common denominators in these two examples of famous people are that even introverted or somewhat shy people or those who initially come across less than charismatic can learn to be more so in situations that demand it. You can, too.

Add Some More "Fire and Lightning" to Your Personality and Leadership Image and Effectiveness

John Antonakis is a professor at the University of Lausanne in Switzerland known for his work on charisma and transformational leadership. A team of management scholars led by him decided to see if they could measurably affect the charisma of a group of middle managers by teaching them a few learnable communication strategies during a five-hour group workshop, followed by a one-hour individual coaching session. After three months, and 360-degree evaluations they received, it showed that the managers who attended the training and applied the techniques were not only perceived as more charismatic, but more trustworthy and competent as well. Here are some behaviors that will, if mastered, make you more charismatic as a person and leader.

One: Smile More. Most charismatic people are warm and approachable. Genuinely smiling more helps in firmly establishing that. A smile conveys feelings of happiness, hope and positivity to anyone who sees it. Yes, there are people who don't smile but are still viewed as charismatic mainly because of the raw force of their personality. But, look at Barack Obama, considered to have the best engaging smile of any charismatic U.S. President and how that brightens his image. Basketball great Magic Johnson has magic in his smile. Dwayne Johnson ("The Rock") is a highly expressive, charming and effusive person, actor and former wrestler. While he can play movie roles looking serious, threatening and intimidating, the second he flashes his huge killer smile, he ignites his warmth, approachability and charisma.

We often feel happier around children – they smile more than adults. On average, they do so 400 times a day. While happy, charismatic people still smile 40-50 times a day, the average of us only does so about 15-20 times. Smiles (and frowns) are contagious — it makes people around you or even in a room feel better because they, consciously or unconsciously, are smiling with you. The simple act of smiling more is an immediate way to ramp up your charisma. Look at most of the famous people you see as charismatic and you'll discover the truth of this.

Two: Be Confident. I mentioned this before and research shows that that real confidence, not arrogance or over-confidence, is attractive in people, especially when situations or experiences might naturally put a dent in one's confidence. Maintaining poise, composure, a relaxed approach, and exhibiting a certain grace under pressure is a catalyst for boosting charisma and admiration from those in whom you come in contact. Confident people have high self-esteem and self-worth and feel comfortable in their own skin without appearing better than others or trying to show how confident they are. You won't find these people bragging, making excuses or needing to be in the spotlight.

Three: Listen, _Really_ Listen. If someone is an empathic, active listener, it's like they turn into a human magnet that immediately draws and keeps people around them, simply because most others are not good listeners, but more interested in their talking. Not only does listening show respect to the person talking, but it also makes that person feel as if he or she is interesting and important. Surprisingly, just listening — what seems like a passive activity — with others makes them see you as charismatic! Asking them questions, getting their opinions and ideas, laughing with them, complimenting people sincerely and otherwise fully engaging them by your rapt listening is most enjoyable and satisfying to people.

Four: Engage People and Make Them Feel Good about Being with You. Any time you approach someone or show deep interest in that person and focus exclusively on them (rather than yourself), they'll see you as "different" — as being charismatic. Give them your full attention, make them feel comfortable and even special and make them the epicenter of your attention. It's often been said that when people met Bill Clinton when he was President or even afterward, that in spite of being on a greeting line of lots of people, he would give that individual great eye contact, a big smile, listen to them in a rapt fashion and project open body language that shouts, "I like you!" They were surprised that they felt a personal connection with Clinton immediately.

Five: Tell Stories That Impact Listeners. There are estimated to be over 10,000 books written about Abraham Lincoln, considered the best US President. Most books highlighted that he was an incredible storyteller, perhaps the greatest in history. Lincoln would disclose fascinating and often humorous stories about anything, delivered in a passionate and expressive way. He had a gift for finding just the right anecdote to vividly illustrate his point and make it both emotionally and intellectually compelling, enjoyable and memorable.

Stories constitute the most powerful weapon in a leader's arsenal," Dr. Howard Gardner, a Harvard University professor and author noted. As an example, in his book, *TED Talks Storytelling*, author Akash Karia studied over 200 of the most popular TED talks by scrutinizing the messages, delivery and composition of each speech. He found that the "magic ingredient" that made those TED talks so compelling was that each speaker mastered the art of storytelling. It greatly added to their charisma. Inside you is a natural-born storyteller waiting to be released. If you can add humor, all the better to boost your charisma. Great stories are timeless. Go for it!

Six: Let Your Warmth Come Through. Most charismatic individuals are genuinely warm and radiant people. Call them friendly, approachable, gracious, engaging and just nice to be around. You won't find warm people being impersonal, aloof, self-absorbed, detached, haughty, guarded or acting superior, even if they are in high positions in their organization. They treat others as equals, even though they may be richer, famous and higher on the social ladder. Making people feel good makes these charismatic people feel good.

Warm people are empathic, compassionate and caring. Research shows that good eye contact, nodding, smiling and genuinely noticing something positive about someone and then complimenting them about it are actually indicators of personal warmth. Being warm means you don't complain, criticize others or otherwise come across judgmental and harsh.

Six: Display Optimism and a Positive Outlook. Charismatic leaders psychologically use optimistic language and focus on a positive "Can Do!" attitude to motivate and inspire people toward peak performance. Instead of being a "Devil's Advocate" telling others why something can't be done, they act as an "Angel's Advocate" to look on the positive side of achieving a challenging goal or a far-out innovation. They draw people into their sphere of influence with their positive and optimistic outlook.

Self-help book author Karen Salmonsohn put it in clear perspective, "Being negative is like spraying yourself with anti-charisma. Pessimism, a bleak outlook and avoiding the "Dastardly D's" — discouragement, disillusionment, dejection, and depression — have no place in the psychological makeup, behavior and communication of charismatic leaders. Their uplifting attitude becomes contagious with their followers. It's not that these charismatic leaders are unrealistic, it's that they know that being hopeful, bullish and bright about possibilities can only help people to achieve things they might have thought unlikely or impossible. So make sure you come across optimistic and positive, especially in tough times when employee morale is sinking, and some feel a sense of despair and defeat.

Seven: Perform Captivating and Compelling Talks. There is no other activity, skill or behavior that can make you appear to be charismatic and even a visionary and innovative leader than giving powerful public speeches and creative business presentations. It can be an incredible accelerant for your career if you have a chance to shine in front of others, especially those with powerful influence.

He was a relatively unknown 42-year-old attractive, athletic-looking Illinois State Senator and US Senatorial candidate before he was thrust into the national limelight and became a rapidly rising star primarily because of his powerful, passionate and polished keynote speech at the 2004 Democratic National Convention. His name was Barack Obama.

Few political careers and presidencies have been more defined by speeches than his that vaulted him into the country's consciousness. During his appearance at the 2004 convention, his oratory was meticulously crafted, beautifully written and theatrically, but sincerely delivered. His charm and charisma exploded on stage and afterward and laid the solid groundwork and credibility for his presidential nomination years later. As President, Barack Obama got even better as a charismatic speaker using humor, stories, examples and metaphors to give punch and pizzazz to his points and messages.

Great speakers focus on having a dominant body language that comes across confident, poised and with power by using diverse and targeted gestures, facial expressions (especially smiles), erect posture and purposeful body movement. Training your voice to be an instrument of your information will add impact to your persuasiveness. Interestingly, a Texas communications analytics company did a study that showed that the sound and quality of a speaker's voice matters twice as much as the content of what they are saying.

Eight: Release Your Energy, Enthusiasm and Expressiveness.

Charismatic people and leaders appear to be dynamos of unstoppable energy. You don't see these people as passive, fatigued or listless. When they walk and talk, they become animated and fully express themselves often in an enthusiastic and even passionate way. They talk a bit louder, never sounding monotone. They get excited and show it about imaginative ideas, interesting potential projects, new opportunities, and when their team or followers achieve something big.

Charismatic people never let their energy level and enthusiasm dip at any time. Every person is enthusiastic and energetic at times. One has enthusiasm for 30 minutes – another for 30 days, but the person who has it for 30 years makes a success out of his or her life. Like a lot of personality and behavior changes, you'll find that "forcing" yourself to be more energetic, enthusiastic and expressive will make it stick, and the results will be most satisfying to you.

Rick Winters, from UPS, is the epitome of energy and enthusiasm. We first worked together on the night shift at UPS. I could not believe the passion he displayed daily. Our operation was large, and when our shift started around 3:00 am, Rick would lead meetings with morning motivations. Daily, he was like a coach giving his team a pep talk going into the championship game. Regardless of the day we had, Rick sent us out to do our jobs highly motivated. Going into one peak season, the "Super Bowl of Delivery Time" for those who work for UPS, I remember him creating theme music we played which included five of the fastest songs I am sure he could find. He even gave each of us a CD of our own if we needed a pick-me-up anytime.

Nine: Show and Communicate Moral Conviction. A leader of strong character who genuinely focuses on moral and ethical issues, fights for them and appeals to followers or employees to "do the right thing" will not only reinforce vital values in your organization but also elevate one's status and charisma quotient. Having courage, tenacity and perseverance and taking risks to be righteous, honorable and upright defines laudable leaders. When a leader communicates, shows and actually lives such core values as courage, integrity, authenticity, humility, respect, dedication, compassion, loyalty, dependability, consistency and others of a positive nature, that contribute to one's charisma as well.

Character and Competence Are More Important than Just Charisma Alone

While this chapter is about how charisma can strengthen one's leadership image and abilities, character is far more important than charisma. A person with an ethical and moral character (with an abundance of positive virtues) makes for a good, decent and honorable human being and leader in business, government or the community.

Nigerian economist, turned author and preacher Peter Ajisafe aptly noted, "Charisma without character is postponed calamity."

George Masi, the former CEO of Harris Health System, one of the nation's largest safety-net organizations, made this observation about character and competency. After you reach a certain level in organizational leadership, the assumption is you are competent. Otherwise, you would not have your job. However, more salient is your character. This is a quality that cannot be compromised. Lack of character left unchecked will kill a team.

There are also those charismatic leaders in business who are narcissistic and self-serving who make their organization "all about them" at the expense of employees and other stakeholders. Imagine, though the power and value of combining charisma, character and competence and how that might enable a person to do great, worthwhile and honorable things to which so many would benefit. That's the ultimate leadership power set!

Omar's Bright Tips

Summary for You to Make a Difference by Developing Your Charisma

1. The simple ways to see if people are typically charismatic: they influence people, are warm and likable and get along with everyone, have a presence and will command a room, can lead others and make them feel comfortable and special about themselves, smile a lot and come across energetic, enthusiastic and expressive.

2. Based on the information in this chapter, do an inventory and analysis of your current charisma behaviors and determine how to boost them.

3. Becoming a more powerful speaker is one of the best ways to come across as a charismatic leader.

4. Even if you are somewhat shy or introverted, you can slowly, but definitely work on ways to become more charismatic.

5. The incredibly simple act of smiling more makes a huge difference in giving you more appeal.

6. Learn from observing and "experiencing" charismatic people you see in movies, TV shows, online videos or those you meet in person. Don't copy them but develop and adapt those types of behaviors and styles that genuinely will fit your unique personality.

7. Remember that while charisma can be quite valuable to you, being of ethical character and highly competent in your field of endeavor and leadership roles are most important.

8. Consider taking acting classes to build your charisma and leadership presence.

9. Work on telling more compelling stories and anecdotes.

Chapter 8

Presence: M.A.D. Leaders Exude It
How to Get and Project This Important Trait and Image

"Executive presence is credibility that goes beyond a title."
– Tom Henschel

Did you ever meet a man or woman and knowing nothing about him or her other than their appearance and initial behavior, you get the immediate feeling this person stands apart and above the crowd and is meant to lead others? That's the "IT" or "WOW" factor called *Presence,* and it's important for leadership and executive development and success. Besides being competent and having other valuable management and leadership characteristics and skills, the phenomenon of presence often determines whose career takes off like a rocket and whose sits on the launchpad with a long countdown. It's been a hot topic in books, videos and high-level training for some time now.

The term called *presence* is much like that of *charisma* (that was covered in a previous chapter) in that both can be very valuable in your personal and professional life, yet the two are often seen as an abstract and mysterious set of behaviors, image and personality. Many of us wonder how these special people somehow marvelously and naturally exude their presence. While presence is not easily defined and described and appears uncanny in some ways, we can see, feel and sense someone having presence when we encounter that person. It's a characteristic that telegraphs he or she is in charge or should be. You can also know fairly quickly when someone doesn't have that "right stuff." In this chapter, we will try to deconstruct the mystery that people have about what presence is and how to develop more of it for yourself.

Whether you call it executive or leadership presence, it is a quality definitely worth cultivating. Presence is one of the most common characteristics shared by most CEOs and other leaders in the military, government or other organizations with that certain substance and style. Interestingly, you can see people with quite different personalities and styles, yet they all have presence — they somehow appear credible, self-assured, capable and supremely confident and composed without being arrogant or self-centered. Most have high emotional intelligence and are authentic, relaxed conversationalists, consummate communicators and good listeners who focus on you in ways that make you feel better after being with them. They magnetically pull you into supporting their goals, plans and ideas, while other unfortunate ones lacking any presence, will struggle to motivate employees to peak performance or get their teams and managers to align and commit to their vision.

Leaders, executives or managers with presence radiate the impression they know where they are going, what has to be done to get there and who needs to be part of the special "band of elites" going on the exciting adventure. They possess *gravitas* — a term that comes from Latin — which is generally understood to mean a characteristic that imparts a dignified demeanor and seriousness to a person or how they treat a subject. Among the Romans, *gravitas* was believed to be vital to the character, roles and responsibilities and ultimately success of those important people in authority. Gravitas may also be viewed as "weight" — the ability of someone to strongly influence outcomes, and it signifies a substance and depth of personality and character.

Think of presence as people having and displaying a positive, special "aura" about themselves. Those who have it, whether they are at a meeting or lunch, on stage performing, participating at a meeting, in court pleading their case, or otherwise interacting with others, have this distinctive quality that is some dynamic combination of appearance, demeanor, attitude, and behavior that makes them shine. It doesn't obviously mean they are better than others, but it says that they simply make a stronger and often immediate professional and personal impression that says they are a clear cut above the crowd. When you have presence, you have a greater chance of making a difference.

Maybe it's their dignified or noble bearing without "putting on airs" or just a remarkable comfort they have with themselves and others. It could be the way they walk in a room or step on stage and suddenly command attention and respect. It's that intangible sense that someone unique, perhaps important or distinguished, has entered and filled it with their "take-notice-of-me" essence.

Presence, like charisma, can give you an advantage in a hiring or promotion scenario. According to a study and survey of 268 senior executives by the *Center for Talent Innovation* in New York, they said "executive presence" — how you appear, act and speak — counts for 26 percent of what it takes to get promoted. Over two-thirds of those executives surveyed said that displaying *gravitas* — poise and calm under pressure, confidence and decisiveness — appears to be the major contributors to the presence formula along with masterful speaking skills, assertiveness, the ability to accurately read people and situations and fine appearance.

People with very different personalities and styles can have different variations of presence. For example, one might have "savoir faire" — a finesse, polish, poise, sophistication, style, charm and smoothness of personality, while others exude presence with a more serious, direct, stronger and "energetic" way of being and acting. Like most other human qualities, some people seen to be born with a natural, "stamp-of-approval" presence without working at it, while most of us can and should enhance our presence. It's how you carry yourself, how you think, what and how you say it, and what you do.

People with presence can connect and engage with others in an authentic manner. It's being very comfortable in your own skin and secure acting in any social or business situation. Though some people who project presence may not appear to be "friendly, warm and fuzzy," they have qualities that engender respect and admiration from those to whom they come in contact. In general, though, many with presence are seen as possessing "warm strength."

Some Descriptor Terms of Presence

To better help you get a handle on this elusive thing called presence, here are some words that can describe how a leader or executive acts, looks and communicates in ways to show presence:

- *Bearing or Carriage.* How a person conducts or carries oneself, including good posture, gestures and body movement that shows a relaxed, comfortable and confident set of body language.

- *Demeanor or Manner.* Typical way of acting and showing an attitude. This may include being gracious, courteous, dignified and socially adroit as opposed to being cold, arrogant, dismissive, argumentative, brash, boastful or other traits or behaviors that hurt one's presence.

- *Decorum or Comportment.* Behavior that shows good taste, propriety, refined etiquette and a sense of appropriateness — conducting oneself in a right, proper or expected way in various dealings and on occasions. Some of these rare people would be seen as classy, debonair, suave or cultured.

- *Substance.* You get the impression these genuine people are "deep," and not "shallow." They come across with integrity, character, humility, consistency, and are usually interesting, perhaps because of their diverse experiences and travels. Their substance is exemplified by their selfless accomplishments in making a difference for others and society.

8. PRESENCE: M.A.D. LEADERS EXUDE IT

Impression-Based and Substance-Based Presence

There are two general types of presence. The first is about how a person makes an impression, especially in the beginning of an interaction, entrance into a group or relationship. That's a perception that people have in the short term that may prove accurate or not. Then, there's the more important form of presence that gives a solid, more lasting and accurate picture of an executive or leader through dealing with or learning more about that person after an extended period of time.

Impression-based Presence involves several factors such as the position, status and branding of the person that precedes them. You first meet a C-level individual, for example, from a big organization and you might feel a bit "star-struck" as if meeting a celebrity or someone who gets lots of publicity on TV or the internet. Presence is automatically "attached" to them usually because of their status. Then, there's the eye-catching appearance of the person.

Research shows that tall, attractive, well-dressed and impeccably groomed men and women of any age, ethnicity and race will have an advantage in the presence game, whether that's fair or not. Third, you see a person interacting and socializing in such a natural and comfortable way, smiling and conversing so smoothly that the presence of him or her just exudes outward. So, this type of presence is about how someone looks, talks, interacts, socializes with grace and ease and makes a great impression right away. While this can be an important factor and a valuable asset, it's really the "surface presence" and may not go deeper with a particular person once you get to know or work with him or her.

The second type, called *Substance-based Presence,* is a longer-term and more reliable indicator of the character and overall "package" of an executive or leader. This involves how people properly and rightfully use power in their position, how they regularly treat people they come in contact with, the quality of relationships with people they work with or occasionally interact with and the ethical values they live by. Finally, this more solid form of presence is shown by the consistent, on-going results, achievements and successes this person has had. This is often called "Earned Presence."

Does a person with charisma have presence and does one with presence have charisma? As I covered in a previous chapter, people with charisma are very engaging, expressive, energetic and interesting and even fascinating and even dazzling. They're approachable and smile a lot and are enjoyable and fun to be around. They are charming and have terrific "people and social skills" with a magnetic quality that pulls others toward them. They can enter a room and light it up like a Roman candle.

A leader with presence may also have charisma. That's a very powerful combination! But, remember that having presence is usually about a more poised, restrained and perhaps dignified persona — someone who might be distinctive and prominent. Movie character James Bond 007 who is well-dressed, strong, intelligent, competent, decisive, composed, sharp, courageous, "classy," and able to mingle and fit in in any social circles had these sublime qualities of a formidable, reserved and regal presence. But, he's not necessarily charismatic.

There is no discernible must have a direct link between charisma and presence, although, like a Venn diagram of two circles intersecting and sharing a common area, there are parts of each blending to some extent with each of us. Comedian Robin Williams — funny, witty, super energetic, quicksilver smart and talented — was a "Whirling Dervish" of hyper charisma, but did not have the "gravitas" to be a senior executive or serious leader of a group. Recent Presidents Ronald Reagan, Bill Clinton and Barack Obama had a fortunate mix of both presence and charisma. Jack Welch of General Electric, Ken Chaenault of American Express, Actors George Clooney and Denzel Washington are just a few of numerous celebrities and business leaders who possess both of those valuable, exclusive qualities.

8. PRESENCE: M.A.D. LEADERS EXUDE IT

Lots of Benefits for You if You UP Your Presence

With presence, people take quick notice of you, without your even trying. You're welcomed and invited to be part of conversations, projects and activities. If you are talking, people perk up and say to themselves, "When this person speaks, I need to listen." When you lead, they follow, and when you propose an idea — even a creative one that others might consider far-fetched —they evaluate it with a positive, open-minded attitude. In every encounter and activity, you stand tall, even if only 5 feet in height. No doubt there are surefire advantages to developing more presence in your personal life and at work.

Each of us has a degree and form of presence that affects how people perceive and react to us. By developing new behaviors and skills and by strengthening those areas you already have in your presence equation, it will help you in social, business and political circles and in your personal relationships. Who doesn't want to make an excellent impression and be able to develop faster and stronger trust, rapport and relationships with others? Developing greater presence is important to those who want to boost their leadership success in business, academia, entertainment, politics, government, the military, science, and so many other fields of endeavor. Here are specific positive outcomes you will likely experience by enhancing your personal and professional presence:

1. Faster career growth, promotability and visibility.

2. Getting more sales, closing bigger deals and otherwise better influencing and persuading others.

3. Increased credibility and respect among top management, your peers, employees and even competitors.

4. Being awarded greater leadership roles and strategic opportunities.

5. Invitations to sit on the boards both for profit and non-profit organizations.

6. Enhanced professional reputation, prestige, status, and standing in your industry and social circles.

7. Being invited to more professional, community and political events and being asked to be a speaker at them.

8. Escalating financial rewards and being afforded new opportunities to make a greater difference and contribution in what you do for others.

9. Bolstered feelings of self-respect, self-worth and self-esteem.

10. Greater impact and success with your business presentations, public speeches, webinars, podcasts, videoconferencing, TV appearances, videotapings and radio interviews.

11. Enhanced ability to lead an organization through innovation, culture and other types of strategic changes.

Presence, like its cousin charisma takes many forms and characteristics of being from mild to strong and from subtle to forthright and blatant. Following are examples of variations and categories of presence that you will see some differences in each style.

Stage Presence

Leaders and executives can learn about presence from actors. That's especially important if leaders give speeches or presentations to large groups. I even recommend that some executives attend acting classes to build their charisma, presence and speaking and storytelling skills. *Stage Presence* typically applies to actors in a live theater performance or to singers, musicians, comedians, magicians or others who entertain audiences with their "expressed confidence." Stage presence is a more active, dynamic and expressive form of presence (combined with charisma), compared to a more subdued version of executive or leadership presence. Stage actors seem to develop and display it more than most TV or movie actors. Those who are tops at stage presence command their audience's interest when they speak. In a CBS 60 Minutes TV program recently, actor Samuel L. Jackson was interviewed and talked about his theatre experience before his film and TV experiences took off, "That when you come on stage, you light it up to the point that when you leave, people want to go with you."

Great theatre and film actors from the past and present like Richard Burton, Vanessa Redgrave, Laurence Fishburne, Laurence Olivier, Viola Davis, John Gielgud, Judi Dench, and James Earl Jones have the creative talent and persona to transform themselves into characters beyond their audience's expectations to deliver totally realistic and memorable performances. Broadway stars can project sheer confidence and naturalness that doesn't seem like "acting," but instead "being." Former President Ronald Reagan would say, "How can a president not be an actor?" He didn't mean for them to be disingenuous, but to use those techniques and skills in a sincere, ethical and true-to-your personality natural way to enhance your ability to influence, inspire and lead.

As I became a more polished and powerful speaker through having had a consummate speech coach and practicing a lot to sharpen my skills and stage presence, I now consider myself a "performer" of sorts because audiences and groups must buy into me before they accept my information, recommendations and requests. Highly successful keynote speakers and especially motivational speakers must be good performers by enlightening, inspiring, motivating, amusing and entertaining their groups. Some of the best have taken extensive acting lessons, and it shows based upon their success.

When you experience an actor or other entertainer on stage with great stage presence, your emotions will be stirred, your attention riveted and your interest assured. Those having stage presence know just how to play with the audience and pull their strings of emotion and thought. They can make you cry or laugh and keep you guessing with curiosity or suspense. It's every performer's job to make it look easy, even effortless and that has required endless hours of demanding practice and experimenting with styles to finely hone their craft. While some are gifted with a natural, inborn stage aura that shines, most of us have to develop it — and you can.

Command Presence Leadership

In today's sophisticated environment, a domineering or authoritative form of leadership or management is shunned upon by employees and followers. However, if your company, organization or government agency, for example, is going through an urgent crisis, major turmoil or upheaval, then a strong, decisive take-charge form of leadership is usually imperative to avoid catastrophe or stem the tide of escalating, out-of-control problems or threats. This is when a leader projects a variation of presence called *Command Presence*. If you are or were in the military, law enforcement, or emergency services where projection of power and authority are important, then you know about command presence.

Command presence is used to take control and charge right away and exert that stronger authority when needed, especially in confrontational, chaotic or emergency situations. Command presence is conveyed by a heightened form of how you *speak*, how you *carry yourself*, how you *appear* and how you *act*. By its very nature and need, it has to be more forceful, direct and authoritative than other forms of presence. This type of strong presence is when you can step in front of a group of individuals and they instantly recognize and know you are the one in charge and can handle the situation effectively.

When a police officer, for example, stops your car for a speeding ticket or suspected crime, he or she must get obedience and cooperation by their presence. The police officer is trained to instinctively adopt a command presence posture through body language, serious demeanor, and strong vocal style to maintain appropriate dominance and mastery over the situation, while appearing confident and powerful. This type of command presence can also be abused by those in positions of authority. Unfortunately, not everyone empowered with command presence is worthy of the honor and respect because of flawed personal characteristics.

Uniforms that are spotless, pressed and tailored to fit well along with professional equipment and impeccable grooming and appearance are prerequisites to attaining this type of presence. "Bad guys" quickly size up officers as to whether they are even slightly tentative, nervous, timid or display the most subtle signs of apprehension or weakness. At that point, violent suspects will likely resist or attack the officer, if they believe they will get the upper hand, while another officer who shows definite command presence will psychologically induce the individual to back down and comply with his or her orders.

Famous World War Two General George S. Patton was usually seen wearing a well-tailored and distinctive uniform consisting of a sharp-looking jacket, highly-polished helmet, riding pants, and high cavalry boots along with his two pearl-handled, engraved silver-plated .357 Smith & Wesson magnum revolvers. It made for an impressive sight designed to inspire his men while garnering respect and fear from his enemies. Patton also cultivated a stern expression he called his "war face." His appearance, his serious demeanor, along with his often direct and "salty language" displayed the epitome of the ultimate command presence warrior-leader who always focused on the offensive. "Presentation" of appearance and behavior is everything in bolstering credibility and command presence, even in a business environment when needed.

How to Develop More of Your Presence

Leadership and Executive Presence come down to building and strengthening four areas: 1. How you act; 2. How you interact; 3. How you look and appear to others; and 4. How you speak and communicate. Here are brief guidelines to help you build or enhance your presence:

1. Show Calm, Composure and Self-Control. Projecting confidence and "grace under fire" was the number one pick in a survey of senior executives that asked to identify what constitutes presence. In a Stanford Business School study that looked at the key qualities that companies look for in promoting managers to senior executive positions, especially that of Chief Executive Officer (CEO) and that of other C-level positions, they identified two important qualities required for great leadership success. The first is knowing how to select and put together a strong team and how to function and lead as a good team player. The other is the knack of functioning well under stress and pressure, especially in a crisis situation. Showing patience, composure and a calm, steady, methodical approach to deal with difficult or disappointing situations is an advantage in getting promoted.

The U.S. Air Force had a stringent selection process with multiple criteria that test pilots for new fighter jets had to meet. So did NASA in selecting astronauts. Extreme physical fitness, education, technical expertise, experience, teamwork and many other standards had to be met to be part of this exclusive, "elite club." But one thing was paramount — the ability to remain calm under even life-threatening situations with a new prototype fighter or spacecraft. It was imperative to be able to deal with a serious problem, malfunction or potential disaster without panicking. Some had that makeup already, others practiced and disciplined themselves on how to adjust their thinking and prevent their adrenalin from spiking. As a potential or current leader, research ways for yourself to be more composed, calm and self-controlled, especially when confronted by emergencies or longer-term high-stress conditions that would causes others to melt down or handle poorly. Research stress reduction programs and even doing deep (diaphragmatic) breathing during the day can often work wonders.

2. **Interact Well with Others.** Leaders and executives with presence focus on the other person(s) and avoid trying to impress others at all costs. Confident and secure, they solidify their presence by the very act of effective listening. There was a recent interview on CBN The 700 Club with James Borrego, the NBA's first Hispanic Head Coach for the Charlotte Hornets. He has a master's degree in leadership from the University of San Diego (USD). In the interview, Borrego said that it's vital to earn the trust of his players and to do that you

must be authentic, "That's really what elevates an organization when there's real, authentic connection and relationship (as a leader)."

The interviewer then asked, "What do you think is the most undervalued when it comes to moving people forward?" Borrego, who is working on his PhD replied, "One of the things I've learned over the years watching great leaders and studying leadership is listening to people, understanding people, empathizing with people. When you listen to them, you value them and when people feel valued, they'll keep coming back to you."

Think about how you typically interact with people and develop genuine ways to improve those interactions through improving your "emotional, social and etiquette intelligence" and behaviors.

3. Ace Your Appearance and Body Language. A study by Harvard Medical School and Massachusetts General Hospital suggests that colleagues size up your competence, likability and trustworthiness in 250 milliseconds (one-quarter of a second!) — based simply on your appearance. Leaders with strong presence wear clothes of high quality, good taste, appropriate to the occasion and well-tailored. Business executives will always have a certain elegant, but understated look that says "well-put-together." Men and women need to avoid anything "glitzy," trendy, or overdone in terms of flashy or lots of jewelry, watches or accessories that detract from a professional look in the executive suite. Impeccable grooming is critical and part of the "well-put-together" formula.

Another key aspect of how you look is your use of body language to project presence. People who smile frequently or have a peaceful and undisturbed facial expression, stand erect with good posture and a relaxed, open body position while gesturing naturally come across well when seen. You won't see successful leaders fidgeting, having their eyes darting around, moving in an erratic way or showing nervous, stressed-out or insecure mannerisms that smack of being uncomfortable or inadequate for the job at hand at the time.

Work on maintaining your top-notch appearance and the body language of poise and power.

4. **Communicate and "Command the Room."** Part of your leadership presence is communicating in a clear, concise and convincing way. At meetings, for example, I've found that impressive executives weigh their ideas, responses and questions carefully before offering them up. I seldom see them "shooting from the hip." Focus on asking very selective, thought-provoking questions that get those in the meeting to see things from fresh, new perspectives so can better solve problems and generate better ideas. Next, work on becoming a compelling and polished public speaker and convincing business presenter. This will skyrocket your presence and image dramatically. Consider joining your local Toastmasters club and hiring a good speech coach to help with your voice and body language techniques, your speech content and even your presentation visuals.

Omar's Bright Ideas

Summary for You to Make a Difference by Strengthening Your Presence

1. Ask a variety of people you respect for candid feedback about how you come across to others in terms of your presence and overall image.

2. Be sharp in how you look, act, and speak. That's how others will perceive and receive you.

3. Dress in a high quality and appropriate way and be groomed as well as you can. While appearance is not everything, it counts!

4. Stand tall with good posture and use relaxed, open body language.

5. Consider taking acting and speaking lessons to boost your leadership presence.

6. Decide when to transition to a command presence posture when needed.

7. Work on developing (or strengthening) a calm, composed and in-control set of behaviors.

8. Continue to enhance your listening, questioning, conversational and overall communication skills. Be selective and ask thought-provoking, interesting questions.

9. Observe others with a great deal of presence and emulate and role model those things that fit within your personality, but don't copy the person.

10. Be aware of and try to eliminate any even minor negative mannerisms or behaviors that come across as exposing you to be uncomfortable, insecure or nervous around people.

11. Leadership is the challenge to be something more than average and having presence will make you stand apart and above others and therefore enhance your leadership abilities and stature.

12. Developing greater presence and charisma is not about being someone you're not — it's about being a better you. Your character is the most important factor that shines and makes a difference in life and at work.

M.A.D.* LEADERSHIP

Chapter 9

Are You a "Cultured" Leader?

Transforming Your Organization's Culture Into a Force Multiplier for Peak Performance and Innovation

"Until I came to IBM, I probably would have told you that culture was just one among several important elements in any organization's makeup and success — along with vision, strategy, marketing, financials, and the like. I came to see in my time at IBM that culture isn't just one aspect of the game, it is the game. In the end, an organization is nothing more than the collective capacity of its people to create value."
– Louis V. Gerstner, Jr., Former CEO of IBM

Today there is a greater emphasis on fully understanding what an organizational culture is, what it does and how it determines and powers an organization's direction, performance, competitive advantage and overall long-term success. What is a "great" culture? What is the "right" culture? How do you leverage it for effect? And what are the roles of the leaders in the culture equation? In this chapter, I'll cover those important questions.

There is no direct financial indicator to measure the strength of a corporate culture, yet it is probably the ultimate differentiator and impetus for long-term, sustainable business performance and supremacy. Make no mistake about it, cultures are M.A.D. — Making A Difference in operations, financial performance and industry standing. Peter Drucker, the famous management consultant and author, put it simply, "Culture eats strategy for breakfast." It's that important for talent attraction, growth, reputation, brand recognition and organizational excellence.

Importance, Purpose, and Value of a Great Organizational Culture

Culture determines how an organization functions. Author and former MIT professor at the Sloan School of Management Edgar Schein, considered the leading authority on organizational cultures, summed it up this way, "Culture is the deeper level of basic assumptions and beliefs that are shared by members of an organization, that operate unconsciously and define in a basic 'take for granted' fashion an organization's view of itself and its environment." The vital importance of having the right culture now and in the future is becoming clearer to leaders than ever before.

With PwC's *Culture and Change Management Survey* of over 2,200 global business leaders done in 2013, they found that 84 percent say culture is critical to business success and 51 percent believe a major overhaul in their culture is currently needed. In an updated PwC survey later done in 2018 of over 2,000 people in 50 countries, 80 percent (increased from 51 percent five years ago) said workplace culture must change. PwC defines organizational culture as an organization's "self-sustaining patterns of behaving, feeling, thinking, and believing – that determine how we do things around here."

From the 2018 study, PwC identified four "critical few behaviors" that will shift one's organizational culture into high gear. They are: 1. Innovative; 2. Collaborative; 3. Customer-centered; and 4. Agile. I agree with those, and I believe those critical factors will shape more cultures in the future. Brian Halligan, CEO of HubSpot added to that when he said, "The way I think about culture is that modern humans have radically changed the way that they work and the way that they live. Companies need to change the way they manage and lead to match the way that modern humans actually work and live. We're trying to re-craft culture in a way that really matches that. I think that 99 percent of companies are kind of stuck in the '90s when it comes to their culture." Make no mistake; cultural transformation is hard work!

Finally, the PwC study shows a perception disconnect in feelings in the workplace with 87 percent (almost 9 out of 10) senior executives and board members feeling pride in the culture, while only 57 percent of employees feel that sense of pride. It's a good idea for organizational leaders to keep a finger on the overall pulse of the organization and not allow themselves to be blindsided by inaccurate feedback or perceptions and false optimism.

A lot of organizational cultures (especially those in technology, energy, education, construction, manufacturing, biotechnology, distribution, healthcare and many types of services) will be defined by a workplace of the future that is connected, collaborative and creative. When you add in the revolutionary, disruptive changes in the next 5-10 years from Artificial Intelligence (AI), robotics, Internet of Things (IoT), 3D printing and quantum computing, where a huge percentage of jobs will become obsolete according to various studies and predictions, the workplaces and their cultures will experience various degrees of upheavals. In his book *AI Super-Powers*, former head of Google China, author Kai-Fu Lee describes the disruptive cultural events taking place in China that he predicts will lead to its dominance in artificial intelligence.

Every corporation, entrepreneurial firm or startup, government agency, military unit or any type of organization or association has its own unique culture. Metaphorically, you might also think of your institutional culture as the "personality and character" of your organization. In their book, *The Science of Story*, authors Adam Fridman and Hank Osatholthoff note that a culture "is a living, breathing organism that emerges from the social and psychological environment within your company." An organization's culture, which consists of deeply imbedded shared values, beliefs, routines and habits, traditions, philosophies, attitudes, assumptions, stories, myths, principles, priorities, and operating norms, essentially boils down to the common notion of "how things are done around here." In a recent article in Harvard Business Review, the authors said, "Culture is like the wind. It is invisible, yet its effect can be seen and felt. When it is blowing in your direction, it makes for smooth sailing. When it is blowing against you, everything is more difficult."

Corporate culture is implanted in every company's goals, structure as well as the company's approach to its employees, customers, suppliers, strategic partners and even their local community. It determines how people work and behave, what priorities they usually focus on, what they are motivated by and what they get rewarded or punished for. Importantly, culture determines and dictates the form, degree and speed of creativity and innovation practiced there. It establishes the norms of thinking, shared learning and even emotional and social intelligence. Where leadership is strong, so is the culture.

Even though a culture most often operates in the background of an organization's operations, it provides a powerful stimulus and advantages leading to superior performance and outcomes. Here are key specific benefits from having a strong, effective and "right" culture, especially one where creative ideas and a focus on relentless innovation dominates:

- Top-line revenues and bottom line profits are maximized.

- Your branding, reputation, prestige and standing in your industry are elevated.

- High employee morale, motivation, and engagement on the job.

- Improved retention of employees and easier recruitment of the best students from universities and top talent from other organizations.

- Holding onto or advancing your competitive edge in your industry despite tough, aggressive competitors.

- Work climate becomes or remains enjoyable, exciting, and satisfying.

- Customers remain deeply loyal and newer, desirable ones come on board.

- Operational effectiveness, efficiency, productivity and quality are continuously improved.

- Reduced errors and re-work.

- Your company is a rewarding place to work and collaborate with highly professional and dedicated people.

- Employees feel a great sense of their mission, purpose and worthwhile meaning in their work and are driven and dedicated to peak performance and exceptional results.

- Every stakeholder—employees, stockholders, suppliers, partners, customers, your community—involved with your organization will benefit from your strong, positive culture.

Difference Between "Culture" and "Climate"

The terms "culture" and "climate" are often used interchangeably by employees, leaders and others connected with the organization. If culture is thought of as the distinctive identity, personality and character of a company that holds it together and governs how people behave (which is fairly fixed and takes time and effort to change), then climate describes the current feelings, emotions, attitudes and perceptions of the people in a group or an entire organization. Sometimes the differences between climate and culture are subtle, while at other times they are stark, especially if the climate continues digging in for a long time, thus affecting behaviors, beliefs and values that are the cornerstones of culture.

Organizational climate deals with how people are experiencing the work environment and atmosphere at any given moment, and it is usually caused by internal or external changes such as business conditions or management decisions that affect the general mood. It can develop quickly based on events, incidents and situations. A particular climate can come about in a team, group, department or division or a company, for example, and this can be created by what supervisors, managers, teams, executives or leaders do. Climate and culture are often connected to some extent and feed off each other.

If a company just had some good things occur like maybe a huge deal that was won, an expanded bonus policy that excites employees, a new CEO or other leader(s) that people have desperately wanted and needed, or an extended period where cooperation and creativity among groups working on great projects that produced exceptional results (that employees were proud of), then a fired-up climate where people feel optimism, a sense of achievement, pride, positivity, excitement and a hoped-for future filled with continued possibilities and opportunities exists.

Conversely, If an unwelcomed merger has happened causing anxiety for many or the company has had several quarters of disappointing revenues and profits that impact job security, or a series of HR policies and restricted budgets are affecting important resources, salaries, bonuses, career advancement opportunities or other aspects of job satisfaction, then the happy-to-grumpy ratio and morale will take a beating. Revenue swings in the company, for example, can affect climate without changing the culture. Employees might feel resentful or despondent that their bonuses were canceled and that their friends were laid off. The culture stayed the same, but the climate changed for the worse.

Currently, in healthcare and many other industries, the lessening supply of competent workers is leading to a more stressful culture. As employees are asked to do more with less, the climate will undoubtably be disrupted and new norms of work must be established. One of the council members, C.O. Bradford, would ask all of the department heads during our budget reviews about the implementation of new technology in our respective areas. As we boasted of our accomplishments, he also asked how we were redesigning processes, given our advancements.

The distinction matters because problems with culture and those with climate are resolved with different solutions. <u>Employee surveys</u> and face-to-face candid interviews and discussions are good ways to get a broad sense of staff members' feelings, attitudes and thoughts so feedback can serve as a springboard for programs aimed at improving those conditions that led to the changed climate.

Types of Cultures. Is There One That Is "Right and Ideal"?

Executives want to know what the "right and ideal culture" is and how can it be shaped and optimized to best meet future needs and challenges their organization will face. It's almost like asking what is the best personality for someone to have? Every culture, like a personality, has its unique characteristics, attractions, strengths and weaknesses. An ideal (good-to-great) culture, though, is essentially one that significantly helps an organization achieve its vision and goals and where superior productivity, efficiency, work excellence and quality of operations and financial performance prevail. The right culture will prepare an organization for "winning" in the future.

If you asked employees or followers, "Do you have the opportunity to do what you do best every day or most of the time?" then, if a large majority of people answered "yes" to that question, it's an accurate indicator of an effective, positive culture and a good predictor of success for the company. A "bad" culture, on the other hand, simply inhibits and prevents workers' peak performance from happening and thus limits how successful the organization and its stakeholders (especially employees) can become.

There could be "subcultures" within an organization that are a bit different than the whole of the culture because managers and leaders in them have a focus and ways of managing and operating that are somewhat different, but not necessarily in opposition to those elsewhere. For example, a sales and marketing group or department might promote and support more creativity and flexibility and have a greater "fun and playful factor" than other departments. The same applies to climate. There might be departments where the climate is positive, and others where the morale is lower and the environment is somewhat toxic. Remember that leaders who role model the values, beliefs, and behaviors in their subculture, set the standard and model for it.

Charlie Brooks, who promoted me from supervisor to manager over my first operation at UPS, would tell us all the time that when there was a high level of employee problems, you would generally find high levels of injuries, grievances, errors and low productivity. The culture was good, but the climate was bad. As leaders working under his leadership, he challenged us to fix the climate.

It is safe to say that with today's unpredictable world in frenetic flux, where technological, political, social, scientific, military and business change can suddenly erupt and cause disruptions (good and bad for someone), then a culture that is agile, creative, responsive, innovative, collaborative, adaptive and flexible to timely change is worthy of most organizations. Dr. Jack Matson, who has taught innovation and "intelligent fast failure," says that to be and remain an innovative industry leader, "one must change faster than change itself." While true, that's quite a challenging, but worthy assignment in today's flurry and turmoil of change.

Some organizations have current cultures that stifle continuous improvement and progress with a rigid bureaucracy and regimen defined by excessive red tape overflowing with hard-nosed policies, rules, procedures and autocratic, command-and-control style of management that dictates with a heavy hand and hard heart. Other organizations and companies have an exhilarating, energetic, results-focused and satisfying work environment with visionary, open-minded, supportive (especially encouraging) and engaging leaders. In these types of energizing cultures, a visitor can "feel the pulse of the place" that is filled with imaginative ideas and eager excitement to innovate and do "amazing things."

These personalities of cultures run the gamut from serious (even stern), restrained, analytical, slow-deciding, slow-moving and ultra-cautious to those on the other end as quicksilver agile, competitive, decisive acting, risk-oriented, optimistic, bold and daring with a sense of spirited adventure and unabashed "can-do-ism."

9. ARE YOU A "CULTURED" LEADER?

Some cultures are conservative and traditional with an adherence to "the way things have been and always are done around here" — by the book with little or no deviation. Innovative and entrepreneurial companies reduce bureaucracy, and, instead, have small numbers of flexible (but critical) guidelines and directions to follow. Red tape is minimized so their creative teams can move fast and sure to deal with suddenly changing technologies, aggressive competitors and an unpredictable marketplace where upstart newcomers are out to grab a slice of market share and keep on grabbing.

Visionary leaders of forward-thinking cultures, who are not afraid to defiantly buck the crowd of me-too imitators in their industry, often encourage and reward the rule-breakers and mavericks who create their teams' spectacular results and quantum leaps because they are, allowed to imagine in a far-out, blue sky way, fail smartly, but learn from it and ultimately do audacious things. Whether a conforming or creative culture (or a mix somewhere between), every organization has DNA in their operations that often reflects what the

company's founder or long-serving top leader espouses and role models.

Companies like Apple, Google, Uber, Airbnb, Amazon, FedEx, SpaceX, Disney, Pixar, Intel, IBM and Microsoft are just some of the corporations that thrive in a culture that honors and rewards as much free thinking and innovation as employees can bring about. There are cultures of innovation in every industry, not just those in high technology sectors. IBM, which is over 100 years old, has a more formal "buttoned-down" culture, although it has loosened up quite a bit in the last twenty years. Their famous company slogan was "Think." Apple and Google have a more informal and playful culture compared to IBM. Apple's slogan is "Think Different" and they do.

Yet, IBM has reinvented itself several times and is a superb innovator and eminently financially successful company. That's likely why it is over a century old (founded in 1911). IBM was the first company to exceed 7,000 patents in a year. It earned a record 9,100 U.S. patents in 2018 that includes a growing number of breakthroughs related to artificial intelligence and quantum computing, which experts see as critical technologies of the future. This was the impressive 26th year in a row IBM has been the top recipient of patents. Its visionary culture focuses on continuous innovation that fuels its prosperity and longevity.

What all exceptional, future-oriented, top-performing companies like IBM have in common is that they consider creativity and innovation to be the lasting, absolutely vital underpinning of their past, present and future successes. Innovation will get an organization out of trouble and keep it out of trouble if it is applied smartly, continuously and assertively throughout the organization.

Core Values — the Bedrock — of An Organization's Culture

If you want to truly understand the heart and soul of an organization's culture, you must start with its *core values*— those that are most central and the most important backbone to it and its operation. The core values are the underpinnings of a company's beliefs, philosophies, principles, priorities and code of ethics for doing business and guiding their actions and conduct. The core values build the brand, and the brand builds the company. They determine what is important to a company and what is good, desirable and worthwhile. They form the essence of cultures. Do you know the core values in your company or organization? Do they align with your personal values?

Core values or guiding principles make a difference in what your organization stands for, what they do and are competent at and even how they want to continue to evolve into in the future. Core values also help companies to determine if they are on the right path and fulfilling their vision and goals by creating an unwavering guide. Cherished values acted upon are really the lifeline of a company if it is to prosper and succeed. Leaders and managers have to role model those values for them to be embedded deeply into the organization. *Here are just a few different examples of core values in some companies. Notice the variety in how they describe or list these shared values.*

9. ARE YOU A "CULTURED" LEADER?

I worked for UPS for 26 years. It was a terrific experience, and I learned so much as an employee, manager and leader. Here are the "Values: Our Enduring Beliefs" that UPS instills in its people:

- *Integrity* – It is the core of who we are and all we do.
- *Teamwork* – Determined people working together can accomplish anything.
- *Service* – Serving the needs of our customers and communities is central to our success.
- *Quality and Efficiency* – We remain constructively dissatisfied in our pursuit of excellence.
- *Safety* – The well-being of our people, business partners, and the public is imperative.
- *Sustainability* – Long-term prosperity requires our continued commitment to environmental stewardship and social responsibility.
- *Innovation* – Creativity and change are essential to growth."

John Deere. *"Our core values define us. They unite us and differentiate us from competitors. Our commitment to these core values is not optional, and never wavers."* Deere defines their four values as: integrity, quality, commitment, innovation.

Ford Motor Company. *Here are the basic core values they list:*

People: Our people are the source of our strength. They provide our corporate intelligence and determine our reputation and vitality. Involvement and teamwork are our core human values.

Products: Our products are the end result of our efforts, and they should be the best in serving our customers worldwide. As our products are viewed, so are we viewed.

Profits: Profits are the ultimate measure of how efficiently we provide customers with the best products for their needs. Profits must survive and grow.

Adobe. Computer software company Adobe has been widely recognized as having a winning culture. That's reflected with their having a superb 98 percent approval rating on Glassdoor, one of the world's largest job and recruiting sites. In 2019, Adobe was recognized in Fortune Magazine's "100 Best Companies to Work For" for the 19th time. Their core values are: Genuine, Exceptional, Innovative, Involved.

American Express. This successful international company states, "Our shared values are Customer commitment, Quality, Integrity, Teamwork, Respect for People, Good Citizenship, A Will to Win and Personal Accountability. By acting according to these values and expecting our suppliers to act accordingly as well, we will inspire the loyalty of our customers, earn a sustainable leadership position in our business, attract and retain a highly talented and engaged workforce, and provide a superior return to our shareholders. This, in turn, will enable us to achieve our vision of becoming the world's most respected service brand."

Zappos (owned by Amazon). One of the largest shoe retailers in the world, this unconventional and wildly and wonderfully creative company learned that culture makes the big difference between success and failure. "We've learned that if you identify your company's core values, hire by them, onboard team members by them, and truly live them, then you can get out of the way. Your team will do the best job for you and be able to provide story-worthy (we call it WOW) service and experiences to your customers." Their 10 core values are:

1. Deliver WOW Through Service.

2. Embrace and Drive Change.

3. Create Fun and A Little Weirdness.

4. Be Adventurous, Creative, and Open-Minded.

5. Pursue Growth and Learning.

6. Build Open and Honest Relationships with Communication.

7. Build a Positive Team and Family Spirit.

8. Do More with Less.

9. Be Passionate and Determined.

10. Be Humble.

Zappos actually has a "Zappos Culture Camp" where they teach other organizations how to power up their culture.

Developing a More Creative and Innovative Culture

Your company's culture is a strong foundation for current and future innovation and creativity. Your leaders' job is to build and reinforce that foundation. Culture powerfully sets the stage for the type, degree and amount of continuous innovation that happens in all areas. It's the "petri dish" of growing great ideas that are implemented or commercialized.

During the 2012 Conference Board CEO Challenge, it was revealed that the top two concerns for CEOs are innovation and human capital, while the top two strategies to deal with them are creating a culture of innovation and applying new technologies (product, process, information, others).

Denison Consulting finalized a study of culture done over 12 years of over 294,000 employees in 664 organizations. They found that 84 percent of innovation effectiveness was explained by four fundamental cultural traits of adaptability, involvement, mission and consistency. While many managers and leaders focus on organizational structure, job characteristics and roles, management processes and strategies and capital as the key drivers of innovation, their study shows that a strong, vibrant culture supporting risk-taking, idea generation and implementation of creative concepts and solutions is the strongest driver of all. So, if you, as a leader, want to have maximum amounts of sustained excellence and innovation over the long run, then your job is to create, nurture and grow a culture where innovation is the main focus in every aspect of your organization's planning, operations, activities, management and organization structure and business model.

Steve Jobs, the founder of Apple Inc., was a multi-billionaire who tirelessly worked as CEO right before he passed away. He didn't work for the money alone, but for the love of being creative and making a difference. He was "innovation personified" making elegant product designs with simple, but powerful functionality and a business model that was unrivaled. He was the master of and role model for an exciting vision and its execution, who created a dynamic corporate culture of innovation that will surely last as long as his famed legacy.

The untold story of Apple, Google, Disney, Pixar, Amazon, Space X, IDEO and other innovative companies is what happens behind the scenes and the amount of experimentation, trial and error, setting up workflows, empowering and motivating employees and deciding on what priority innovation projects in which to bring to success. Culture is the mechanism to make it all happen — behind the scenes. And behind are those employees with curiosity, passion and the desire to explore novel, unconventional and even outlandish, far-out ideas that can cause breakthroughs and even quantum leaps.

One of the most important ways to craft a culture of innovation is to remove or at least minimize barriers, obstacles, counterproductive politics, red tape and, especially, a burdensome bureaucracy full of restricting and unnecessary rules, policies and procedures. That's exactly what Arthur C. Martinez did when he became CEO of Sears in 1996. He reengineered the corporate culture, which, at the time, contributed to the company's failing performance. Martinez made managers accountable for how well their particular areas performed. Sears had a rigid command-and-control structure where almost everything was decided for them in a gigantic 29,000-page manual of rules and procedures.

9. ARE YOU A "CULTURED" LEADER?

He tossed the massive 29,000-page manual out and instead summarized key operating and leadership guidelines into three documents: 1. "Freedoms and Obligations" was a brief document only about one-eighth of an inch thick; 2. 16-page booklet covering key leadership principles for executives and managers; 3. 17-page code of business conduct for every employee that provides them with priorities to focus on the customer and team members. "We wanted Sears to be compelling to work for, to shop at, and to invest in," Martinez explained in his autobiography. While in the end, he was not able to save Sears, his leadership extended the life of the organization by creating new cultural norms.

Pixar, a world-leading animation studio (a subsidiary of Walt Disney Studios) produced 21 feature films and has earned 19 Academy Awards, 8 Golden Globe Awards and 11 Grammys among other awards as my book is being written. They are considered to have one of the most creative and passionate cultures that thrives on innovation and excellence in design and storytelling. Pixar has a set of leadership beliefs that are the deep underpinnings of its culture. One of the primary leadership roles is to enable and support others to do their best work, rather than telling them how to do it. Leaders focus on promoting soft skills involving team collaboration and improvisation of ideas.

The Pixar culture tolerates lots of ambiguity before ideas are crystallized into valuable outputs. They realize creativity takes time, and quick results are most often not good results. Pixar culture is all about team collaborations that spark brilliant ideas, not mandates from the top management. It's not about great ideas from an individual (or even a "sole genius"), but all about great, diverse creative teams. Pixar co-founder Ed Catmull says, "If you give a good idea to a mediocre team, they'll screw it up. But if you give a mediocre idea to a great team, they'll make it work." It's about the hundreds or even thousands of little, incrementally better ideas that overflow and come out of the team that makes a winning film.

Their culture promotes, supports and encourages building teams that are not only diverse in gender, race and other characteristics, but they also hire and utilize people who are off-beat, free-thinking, even wacky creative personalities who will "rock the boat and shake the trees" to generate breakthroughs, unique concepts, stories and ideas no one has thought about before. Pixar's innovative leaders promote a culture where work is challenging and mentally and emotionally enjoyable and where fun, with its playfulness, laughter, goofing off, cutting up at times releases endorphins and other brain chemicals that cause creativity to overflow.

Apple is always highlighted for its product excellence, innovation and exceptional corporate culture. Their core value is *to make the best products and focus on a few selected ones that they can develop and innovate in ways that give them a consistent competitive advantage.* These core values and operational focus form their corporate culture, the glue of which holds the company together and makes it prosperous and eminently successful.

Apple's employees and leadership believe their important mission is to make truly great products that change lives and change the world. They are dedicated to making a difference — a big difference. Their other cultural value is to avoid the complex and make products and services elegantly simple, giving them an exceptional value proposition. Apple's culture enables their creative people to concentrate on a few vital innovations truly meaningful and important to their vision and mission, instead of diluting their effectiveness by working on thousands of projects, trying to be all things to all people. It's not a slogan with them, but a convicted way of life as they will not settle for less than excellence from every group and team in the company. What helps innovation spread throughout Apple is their extensive, committed collaboration and cross-pollination of their groups that allows them to be creative and innovate in ways others do not.

9. ARE YOU A "CULTURED" LEADER?

Valuable Questions to Help You Assess and Upgrade Your Culture

While there isn't a "Company Culture 101 Blueprint" for every organization to create and follow, you can uncover the unique culture pillars of your organization with the detailed questions that follow. One of the initial steps in improving and sculpting your culture for better performance and overall effectiveness is to identify, analyze and evaluate those aspects that are both strong and weak and then work to reengineer or fine-tune your culture as needed. You can do this by carefully thinking about and answering these questions yourself and also posing these questions to other leaders and employees in your organization and reviewing their feedback. The answers will intuitively, if not obviously, tell you the general nature of your current culture and climate and suggest where gaps exist that you and others should close.

1. How would you describe the general culture of your organization? What descriptive words and terms would you use to sum up the essence of it?

2. On a scale of 1-10 (10 being extremely so), how "excellent" for its employees, customers and other stakeholders do you think your company culture is right now? Describe why you rate it that way.

3. What are the most positive, beneficial aspects of your culture and how do people respond to them and perform as a result?

4. What is the climate right now, and what factors might have brought it about? If there are negative and counterproductive characteristics, what effect is it having on managers and employees?

5. How would you describe the main beliefs, philosophies, principles, attitudes, assumptions, preconceptions and operating norms that affect how people think, act and perform at work in your company? Which ones psychologically affect the behavior of most people and how?

6. What work activities and projects are most challenging, enjoyable and satisfying to most employees regardless of whether they receive recognition or rewards from doing them?

7. What are the most undesirable aspects of your company's culture that negatively affect people's performance, cooperation, and desire to work in your company? What specific impact have these had on operations, goals and accomplishments? Which ones are the most harmful and why?

8. What are the critical core values that drive the actions and performance of employees and managers in your company (e.g., diversity, accountability, teamwork, pursuit of excellence, open communication, integrity, boldness, accountability, innovation, quality, constant improvement, fun)? Do any values have unintended consequences on how employees work together and, if so, what are they?

9. How would you gauge your organization's culture regarding creativity and innovation: non-existent, weak, "average" or strong, and why do you feel that way and what specific evidence do you have?

10. What makes many people generally insecure, concerned, fearful or unhappy about in their jobs or work environment? What impact does it likely have?

11. What typically boosts or hurts morale in your organization?

12. What would you say motivates most people to be highly engaged in your group or organization? What demotivates or prevents people from taking more initiative at work?

13. What behaviors and accomplishments generally get people promoted faster and higher than others?

14. How does your organization deal with change? Historically, what's been the resulting consequences and impact? What drives change, and who typically initiates and drives it? How is change planned and executed?

15. Who would say are the most successful, respected and admired people in your company and why are they considered so?

16. Regarding your company's "relentless focus on customers and service excellence to them," on a scale of 1-10 (10 being "outstanding"), what score would you give your company and why?

17. How are extraordinary efforts, results and "success" recognized and rewarded? How are setbacks and failures addressed?

18. How would you describe the overall communication process in your organization? To what extent is it frequent, open, honest, frank, positive, and supportive versus infrequent, closed, selective, adversarial, or top-down driven only?

19. What are most people tired of, overwhelmed by, or frustrated and annoyed with in your organization and how do they react?

20. What typically drives people to excel at their jobs in your organization? Why would people show initiative to accomplish things? Why might others remain passive and not take the initiative (especially if they had done so in the past)?

21. If you took a poll of most employees in your organization, what percentage might agree that their work was challenging and meaningful in a positive, motivating way? Enjoyable, satisfying and even fun? If you asked people, "What percentage of your true potential are you using on the job?" what would be the most common answers from most?

22. On a scale of 1-10, how supportive is your culture to experimentation and risk-taking and why do you feel that way?

23. What are the real motivating factors that regulate whether there are mostly individual or team projects?

24. What specific bureaucratic rules, procedures, norms, methods, and management behaviors inhibit better performance and results? How can they be eliminated, minimized, or modified? What is holding your company back?

25. How would you describe the general management style throughout your business? What do they do well and are competent at? What should they do better to improve relationships with employees, better motivate and encourage them, be more open to ideas and recommendations and give them more opportunities to excel at work?

Answering these questions can give you more insights into how your organization collectively thinks and acts. Understanding what your culture is now—and how it needs to evolve—will help you map out a way to produce even higher levels of performance in your organization, whatever its size and makeup may be.

Omar's Bright Tips

Summary for You to Make a Difference by Enhancing and Leveraging Your Culture

1. Realize that your organization's culture — that operates in the background — has a huge effect on its operations, employees, other stakeholders and its overall success.

2. A company's culture was often developed by the founder(s) and later supported by and modified by other managers and executives. Core values are the foundation of a culture. Do all of your employees know what they are and do they, along with your company's leaders, behave in accordance with them?

3. Have you assessed your culture lately by asking the types of detailed questions in this chapter?

4. Changing a culture is very difficult and time-consuming but needs to be done if the organization is faltering over an extended period of time and the culture is mainly responsible.

5. In today's faster-than-ever changing, highly-competitive world, an organizational culture that embraces creativity, innovation, and continuous improvement is one that is ideal.

6. Think about what simple aspects of your culture can be enhanced or changed relatively quickly and easily in ways that will improve your operational and financial results.

7. Your leaders are responsible for sustaining a great culture or modifying and enhancing it when needed.

Chapter 10

Your B-I-G And Bold Vision

Be the Visionary Leader Who Creates an Exciting Innovative Future for Your Organization

"Leadership is the capacity to translate vision into reality."
– Warren Bennis

Are you a *visionary leader* or do you feel you want to be one? Do you think and act innovatively to shape the future of your organization? Simply put, visionary leaders create a clear picture of a positive future state. In this chapter, I'll cover information on how you can not only create and communicate a captivating vision for your organization but provide valuable insights on your being more of a visionary leader — someone who communicates an inspiring vision and lives it and role models it day-to-day. Regardless of the type and size of your corporation or company, startup firm, government agency, military unit or any other organization, the vital role of leadership is to provide a future vision that translates into what your organization can, should and will become under your leadership.

However, before I go any further, let me tell you how my thoughts on leadership vision changed over the course of one month. On November 30, 2016, my mother texted me from a routine optometrist visit. She had been telling me for a few weeks she believed that she needed cataract surgery and was going to have her eye checked. Around mid-morning, while I was in a meeting, I received a text from her. The text was short and simply said: "totally blind in the left eye."

Not knowing what to do, I left work and headed to the doctor's office, and he confirmed that due to a lack of blood flow to her optic nerve, the light had gone out and she would not regain sight in her left eye. He showed us the scan of both eyes and the damage that had been done. He told us it would be important to take care of the one good eye and after a few hours of trying to rationalize the situation to my mom, we drove home.

Two weeks later, on December 15th, my mother called me again and told me that she thought we needed to get to the emergency room because of difficulties seeing out of the right eye. My mom spent the next four months in hospitals, rehab and skilled nursing facilities, never regaining her sight after 74 years. On the day she was discharged and sent home, I had no idea how we were going to make it. I realized it would be tough but did not recognize the complexity of the most routine task. Vision, as we all know is both literal and figurative.

A thrilling, spellbinding vision can change the world. Dr. Martin Luther King, Jr.'s dream inspired millions, and President John F. Kennedy's "out-of-this-world" vision got men landing on the moon. Great visions have great power to do great things. Without a clear, purposeful vision, though, an organization and its people will be rudderless — without a direction and sense of meaning. In Proverbs 29:18 in the Bible it says, "Where there is no vision, the people will perish." Helen Keller became deaf and blind at 19 months of age. This incredible human being was made famous in the movie *Miracle Worker*. How she physically, mentally, intellectually and spiritually overcame her condition and what she accomplished is really beyond comprehension. She profoundly and pointedly said, "The only thing worse than being blind is having no vision."

Throughout my book, I've been focusing on the critical need for more transformational leaders — extraordinary people — who will navigate and innovatively lead their organizations through a dangerous gauntlet and whirlwind of global technological, societal, economic and political change. Maintaining the status quo is no longer an option for any organization facing frenetic and often disruptive change. Standing still and doing what you've always done— even though it worked great before or even now — will not ensure long-term survival, let alone the ability to thrive. Part of being a special transformational leader is taking on the role of an innovative visionary – being able to not only see the future more accurately than others but also to *create* an ideal one for your organization. Winston Churchill said, "The empires of the future are empires of the mind."

Transformative leaders with vision who want to make a huge impact will innovate, invent, create, build, and improve every aspect of their organizations. Those intentional leaders who propose bold, daring, outrageous ideas, imaginative goals, wild solutions and far-out dreams might be laughed or scoffed at in the beginning, but these exceptional and courageous pioneers, trendsetters and "overcomers" prove the doubters and cynics wrong by building a brighter future and bringing change in the world by doing things that seemed beyond the bounds of possibility to most others. History shows us that if you can see it, you can make it happen, or as Walt Disney put it, "If you can dream it, you can do it."

You need both a short-term and long-term vision that sets a standard of excellence, clarifies direction and bridges the present to the future. Where do you want your organization to be in the next 2-5 years. This short-term vision can be more achievable and take advantage of current market conditions and evolutionary technologies. A longer-term vision from 5-10+ years is more difficult to realize, but if you plan it well, you can capitalize upon revolutionary technologies and new business models to give your organization a potential leap ahead in your industry.

Employees don't get emotionally revved-up when the CEO only coldly talks about the projected financial future of the company as if that were his or her vision. They need something more that touches their souls and makes them yearn for something of deeper human value and experience. Antoine de Saint-Exupery, a French poet, aristocrat, journalist and pioneer in aviation indirectly addressed vision when he said, "If you want to build a ship, don't herd people together to collect wood and don't assign them tasks and work, but rather teach them to long for the endless immensity of the sea."

There's a brief story that illustrates how some exceptional people perceive their job in a more fulfilling way — they envision the future outcome:

Three men were laying bricks. The first one is asked, "What are you doing?" He replies, "Just laying these bricks all day long!" The second is asked the same question and he replies, "Doing this tough, grinding work so I can feed my family." The third one when asked what his job was, smiled proudly and said, "I'm part of this construction team building a beautiful cathedral so families can come and worship God and feel at peace and harmony."

I have had the honor and privilege over my career to have incredible accomplishments attributed to my leadership. These include physical structures Gregory Lincoln Historical Museum, affordable housing (CCPPI), historical preservation and municipal infrastructure for savings of hundreds of millions of dollars in healthcare costs. Each one of these accomplishments started off with a vision. And, even if I were not leading and only a participant, each accomplishment made a difference to the lives of the people affected. Let me tell you about one that was born out of necessity.

In 2011 the city faced a 50 to 70 million dollar budget deficit. Healthcare costs already at 300 million per year were estimated to increase 30 million dollars if no actions were taken. The Mayor tasked me and my team with looking for ways to rein in cost. Four years later through a more robust wellness program that improved the health of employees and families, improved partnerships and through a better contract management program, we had saved 42 million dollars and costs avoided were a staggering $275 million. The entire vision was started on the simple, common sense premise that healthy people cost less than sick people.

10. YOUR B-I-G AND BOLD VISION

Purpose and Benefits of a Leader's Compelling Vision

A compelling *vision statement* and *vision description* (which is more detailed and valuable) have several important goals and advantages that will help a number of stakeholders (managers, employees, investors, suppliers, partners, volunteers, others) involved with your organization. Most importantly, vision is crucial to setting ambitious and consistent goals and strategies. How can you develop a roadmap if you have no destination in mind?

Painting a shared, uplifting vision that connects with the personal values of employees will help to excite them about your future and inspire and motivate them to act in ways to get to that beckoning point over the horizon. It also enables your HR department and others to decide on what types of people to hire and promote. If everyone is aligned and focused on a worthwhile vision, then it minimizes, if not eliminates departmental silos and fiefdoms and self-serving agendas that pit one functional area against another.

A defining vision can strengthen your culture by giving it a unified purpose to fulfill a bold agenda and a rallying cause and mission for people to embrace. With that new or improved vision, your culture can, therefore, justify creating a framework for new values, policies, principles and empowerment behaviors needed to make the vision a reality. A well-done vision will guide management's thinking on what priority directions, strategies and investments to make, how to best deal with competition or potential challenges and threats, and handle problems to get back on track. Your vision will help solidify what types of overall organizational changes, innovations and opportunities must be pursed. Finally, a stimulating, solid vision will give wings to your innovation plans, branding and prestige.

Every department in your organization will benefit from having its own unique vision — a "sub-vision" — that is supportive of and carefully aligned with the overall vision of the whole organization. Those people managing smaller units in the company should work with their teams to articulate a worthwhile vision they strive toward reaching. It might be a vision for the next year, three years from now or even longer.

Do You Have a Personal Vision for Your Life?

Famous actor Al Pacino said, "If you feel what you are doing is on line and you're going someplace and you have a vision and you stay with it, eventually things will happen." He's right. Regardless of your age or status in life, through your vision, planning and hard work, you can achieve a personal and professional future you desire. If you accurately and frequently visualize (in great detail) exactly what you want to happen in the months or years ahead, your subconscious mind will actually bring your dreams and visions to fruition. Have you developed a detailed vision for your life over the next 3, 5, 10, 20 or more years? It might involve these aspects, for example:

- The extra education or training you want

- Aiming for the job or career that will be wonderful for you in the years ahead

- How you picture yourself volunteering to make a difference

- Getting your "ideal" mate and building a family (or extended family)

- How you see yourself traveling and where. What do you see yourself sightseeing, visiting and learning about? What new types of fun would enrich your life?

- Where you want to live in the future — city, suburbs near mountains and lakes or near the ocean, for example? What does that location look and feel like?

- The type, design and decoration of your future house(s), type of landscape and yard(s). Visualize every aspect of your future home(s) — the rooms, furniture, decorations. Maybe you want two homes, each in a different location.

- How you see your social, political or religious aspirations in life being fulfilled.

- Your desired future leadership roles at work, in church, in your association(s), in politics and elsewhere.

- How will your appearance and dress change (lose weight, gain it, exercise more, tone or build muscle, wear more expensive, higher-quality clothes you will afford)

- The type of new friends you would love to be with.

- What vehicle(s) you will be driving in the years ahead.

- The entertainment, sports, physical or other activities or hobbies in which you see yourself being involved.

- Overall, how will you and your life change and get better as years progress?

Ten Ideal Qualities of a Powerful Vision

If you want people to be genuinely excited about and committed to your vision, here are 10 characteristics that will build a memorable and emotionally and psychologically affecting one:

1. Bodacious. Your vision should stretch boundaries and comfort zones and enable people to realize what could be. So, make your "stretch vision" sufficiently bold, daring and ambitious beyond what you might think is presently possible. You're not aiming so high, that it will be unachievable, but high enough it will challenge everyone. Famous filmmaker James Cameron (with *Alien, Terminator, Titanic, Avatar*) who always pushes the boundaries of movie-making with over-the-top technology, artistry, and storytelling, has this philosophy, "If you set your goals ridiculously high and it's a failure, you will fail above everyone else's success." By the way, "bodacious" is an interesting term that means audacious in a way considered admirable. Try it!

2. Clear and Vivid. Your vision should be crystal clear to your employees or followers. They should be able to thoroughly imagine what an ideal future looks like. One way to do that is to write a detailed description (not just a statement) and perhaps create a multimedia presentation with video, animations and even virtual and augmented reality.

3. Optimistic and Promising. People will feel a sense of hope for something better than it is now where various groups of people at work, your customers, the community and even society will benefit in the future because of your realizing a shared vision for all. The vision should be a rallying point for all concerned.

4. Motivating and Galvanizing. A well-crafted vision will deeply inspire, encourage and push and pull people to support it over the years, even in tough times. The right vision gives people a defined worthwhile mission and cause to work and fight for.

5. Ignite Emotions and Strengthen Relationships. The vision creatively developed and communicated will appeal to the heart, not just mind and foster strong, positive feelings of pride, accomplishment, worth and the sense it will make a difference for many people in many ways. It should stir passion, uplift and invigorate people and create a sense of unity and fellowship in your organization.

6. Exciting. Your vision should feel like going on an invigorating journey and thrilling adventure from now to your appealing future.

7. Value-Focused. Your organization has key values it cherishes, lives by and broadcasts to others. Your vision should include those values along with perhaps new ones that strengthen your organization's guiding principles, posture and ethics.

8. Intentional. What good is a vision without concentrating on the worthwhile purpose, the "obvious why" and tangible benefits behind it? It should provoke, drive and accelerate superior performance regularly in your organization.

9. Shared and Memorable. Craft a compelling vision that people connect with, buy into, share it with others and support it daily. It's *their* vision, not just one which was scripted by those in the C-suites and boardrooms. They must have a sense of ownership in it.

10. Challenging. Your vision should seem out of reach at first thought. It should be an invitation to greatness, to overcome major barriers, obstacles and setbacks. A stirring vision should stretch one's imagination and seem difficult-to-impossible to achieve were it not for the people supporting it with all they have. Jonathan Swift, author of *Gulliver's Travels*, accurately noted, "Vision is the art of seeing what is invisible to others."

What to Consider When Crafting Your Short and Long-term Vision

As a visionary leader working with a group of smart, creative people to help brainstorm items that will assist in developing a final vision for your organization, here are thought-provoking recommendations to consider:

1. Think and dream really B-I-G, but "somewhat realistic." Don't hold back. As I said before, what might seem impossible now could be achieved in the future with the right technology, great teams, smart strategies, new resources, innovative leadership and aggressive project management.

2. Brainstorm bold and daring ideas with a diverse group of your people at all levels in your company and even those outside it such as with customers, suppliers, consultants and others with imaginative ideas, successful experiences and who are good at predicting major trends and changes. Vet the draft vision and make sure it is the right one for your organization.

3. A vision is a work in progress. Think about where your organization should be in the near-term and in the future — 3, 5, 10 or more years onward. Every vision needs modification and revision at some point. Be flexible and

adaptable as you project where your company, division or department should be.

4. Your vision should "emotionally charge" your employees and inspire and motivate them to peak performance. So, design your vision to engage, challenge, activate stimulate and propel people to exceptional action and have them do "amazing things."

5. Ask how your vision can be truly altruistic in terms of helping others, contributing to society, solving an important problem or otherwise doing good and improving the quality of life for people. For example, Apple uses 100 percent renewable energy in its newest buildings and recently announced it has nearly doubled the number of suppliers that have committed to run their Apple-specific production on 100 percent renewable energy.

6. When highlighting your vision, use colorful, descriptive words, images, videos and animations that paint an enticing, hoped-for future and stimulates and stirs people's imaginations and emotions.

7. Think about what values, operating norms, beliefs, assumptions, policies, principles and other elements need to be preserved in your culture and what needs to be changed or new values added when transforming your organization through your vision.

8. Strive to "engineer" your vision so your company can leap ahead of your competitors and innovatively "disrupt" your industry.

9. Research and analyze the types of innovations that likely need to occur or mature to make your vision a reality? You'll need to project how technology, science and other advancements will be in the years ahead.

10. Ask yourself what future problems, threats, challenges will likely present themselves that your organization must deal with and overcome for you to reach your priority strategic goals.

11. Your vision must be highlighted and communicated weekly by managers and executives in subtle or indirect ways.

12. Remember what your organization must do to meet the next milestone heading toward your vision's destination. Every accomplishment, small or large, should contribute to a closer reach of your vision.

Simple Vision "Statements"

Your well-crafted *vision statement* is a concise, simple representation of a desired future reality based upon the type of work and focus of your organization. This brief sentence or paragraph is typically used in websites, social media sites, media interviews, podcasts and other areas of communication. Your *mission statement* differs because it answers *what* your organization does, *who* benefits from it and *how* you accomplish your current work. Some companies and organization mistake one for the other in describing them.

While vision statements have some value as a quick reminder and guidepost for stakeholders, an encapsulated statement alone — without a more detailed and vibrant description of a longed-for and planned future — is often not enough to paint a full, rich picture of excitement to be experienced in the years ahead. But organizations should carefully script a worthy vision statement. Here are examples of real vision statements:

Amazon: "Our vision is to be earth's most customer-centric company; to build a place where people can come to find and discover anything there might want to buy online."

Caterpillar: "Our vision is to a world in which all peoples' basic needs — such as shelter, clean water, sanitation, food and reliable pointer — are fulfilled in an environmentally sustainable way and a company that improves the quality of the environment and the communities where we live and work."

Harley-Davidson: "Harley-Davidson, Inc. is an action-oriented, international company, a leader in its commitment to continuously improve our mutually beneficial relationships with stakeholders (customers, suppliers, employees, shareholders, government, and society). Harley-Davidson believes the key to success is to balance stakeholders' interests through the empowerment of all employees to focus on value-added activities."

IKEA: "At IKEA our vision is to create a better everyday life for the many people. Our business idea supports this vision by offering a wide range of well-designed, functional home furnishing products at prices so low that as many people as possible will be able to afford them."

Tesla: "To create the most compelling car company of the 21st century by driving the world's transition to electric vehicles."

Zappos: "The vision of Zappos.com, is 'delivering happiness to customers, employees, and vendors.'" And their *mission statement* is to "provide the best customer service possible. Deliver WOW through service."

Some vision statements are unusually succinct — one sentence — and quite general (even abstract) in their description. Here are examples:

Alzheimer's Association: "A world without Alzheimer's."

Make-A-Wish Foundation: "That people everywhere will share the power of a wish."

Example of a Detailed, Very Comprehensive Vision Description

Creating detailed vision descriptions or "stories" are more important and valuable than a brief statement that leaves little to grab onto and work toward. The following is a made-up, fabricated detailed vision description of a company somewhat modeled after a real one. As you read it, ask yourself if this vision description would inspire you if you were an employee, investor, or someone who is currently or will be a stakeholder with the *WarpX Motors Corporation*, that is depicted by me as a highly innovative company currently with over

10. YOUR B-I-G AND BOLD VISION

1,000 employees with an expectation to grow by 50 to 100 percent each year. Here is their vision description:

"At WarpX Motors Corporation we intend to electrify the world with our game-changing, disruptive super innovations and it will benefit billions of people around the globe. In the next 10 years, WarpX Motors Corporation will reinvent the electric motor, develop radically new energy storage and distribution systems and develop motors so big they will power the largest jetliners and so small they will pass through human arteries and veins. Our superconducting, multi-axis electric motors will seem the realm of science fiction because our engineers and scientists will make them 20 to 50 times more powerful, 5 times smaller with the same power and able to last 50 years while being 90 percent more efficient. We envision engineering totally new energy technologies and sources, that will make even the most advanced "batteries" seem ancient. They will have 1,000 times the power density of current ones, can be regenerated in minutes and weigh just a fraction of the lightest, highest-density batteries available right now. The energy sources will be 100 percent recyclable.

Our super motors and incredible power sources will revolutionize cars, trucks, ships, trains, aircraft, motorcycles, and construction machinery. They will transform healthcare, electronics, gaming, photography and filmmaking, drones, entertainment activities and amusement rides, prosthetics, appliances, tools, robotics, weapons and thousands of other products and markets. Our quantum leap motors and energy devices and storage systems will help to usher in a super-clean, safe environment that will turn back climate change, open up entire new industries and jobs and foster development of incredible new products and services that only previously existed in the rich imaginations of dreamers — products that will positively affect the safety, health, prosperity and quality of life of people . We will lead that charge to change technology, business and the world. We will make history. Right now, we have three locations in North America. We plan to have about 75 more around the globe in 10 years with revenues that will increase by over 1,000 percent with generous profit-sharing and extensive career training expanded for all employees.

The way we will bring about this significant change and benefit to society is just as creative. Our approach is to work with DARPA, several giant U.S. government laboratories with the world's best scientists and engineers, top universities that have had great success in producing breakthrough prototypes and by collaborating with the most amazing minds on the planet. Our business model will continue to be unlike any others in that we will take big, but smart risks, tap into open innovation companies, unleash and empower our best innovators and leaders, experiment and test using the latest technologies, material sciences, 3D printing and equipment and reinvent our manufacturing to ensure quality that approaches perfection. That amazing horizon might be closer than you think.

We will continue to listen to all ideas from everyone and everywhere, however far-out and outrageous. We will try things and fail but learn from them and never penalize a worthwhile effort that did not pan out. We will greatly value and make best use of our employees, strategic partners, suppliers and other stakeholders, knowing we cannot do amazing things by ourselves. And we will always appreciate, recognize, acknowledge and reward achievements —and even worthy efforts — in pursuit of our vision to electrify the world, literally and figuratively."

Bringing Vivid Life to Your Vision through the Wonders of Digital Magic

Carefully crafted words by a team of imaginative wordsmiths can paint an enticing picture of the planned future of your organization. But there's an even better way if you choose to do it and can afford it — a "Digital Multimedia Story" using the latest 3D animation and motion graphics software (for example LightWave, Maya, Cinema 4D, Mocha AE, Houdini). These amazing, but very complex software programs can create the most realistic-looking scenes, people, cityscapes, objects, water and anything else you see in life. Think of the incredible special effects you see in movies. You can do wonders even with using a talented student in your city's art institutes that teach such digital software. With video, voice narration, 3D animation, photorealistic images and illustrations, perhaps with virtual reality and augmented reality for some applications, people can "see and feel and experience" how your organization or corporation will look like, operate and be transformed by your visionary leaders. It's light years ahead of a vision statement!

Imagine the entrepreneurial mayor of a mid-size city talking about and then showing a 4-minute computer-generated vision of how her city will look like in 10-15 years. It depicts more gorgeous parks, greenways and people walking and biking along paths along a delightful Riverwalk with restaurants and stores. The viewer sees a flyover and views sleek, ultra-modern, sustainable energy buildings, new entertainment venues, artificial waterfalls and beautiful, lush landscapes with impressive moving creative sculptures that abound throughout the "new city." There's innovative, ultra-efficient lighting technology that changes colors and intensity to alter moods and provide spectacular lighting that can be focused anywhere.

In the multimedia animated vision, one can see intersections of "intelligent roads" that guide driverless electric cars, buses and other vehicles safely and efficiently. Shown is a maglev (magnetic levitation) people mover and trains as if in a science fiction movie, but it's part of the vision's real plan for the city. What follows is a virtual flyover (as from 1,000 feet high) giving viewers a stunningly realistic higher altitude "tour" of the futuristic cityscape and the impact it has on the quality of life of its citizens.

Throughout the animated digital vision, you can hear the sounds of birds and nature, waterfalls, cars moving and happy people talking, walking and riding bikes and having fun. This digital technology to make a vision seem so lifelike and believable is available today to create a convincing reality "experience" for your vision. Now, with awesome evolving technologies like

3D holography that will likely be available in 5-7 years the possibility to envision what seems like something out of the realm science fiction will explode the possibilities of compellingly and accurately communicating the future you, as a leader envisions for your organization.

Making the Vision Come Alive Through Your Visionary Leadership

You need to bring your vision to life, make it part of your culture, your communications, marketing and branding. What good is coming up with a great vision and not frequently capitalizing upon it? Just putting it on your website or occasionally in your publications and referring to it several times a year will not make it stick or stand out. If you've spent the time to be creative in crafting your vision, why not be creative in how you highlight, showcase and reinforce it and have people sharply focus on it a regular basis. Here are a few ways for you as a visionary leader to keep your vision on center stage and in the minds and hearts of people:

- Make sure you get a diverse group of people in your company or organization to provide input for the vision to make in a "shared vision" that gets widespread support.

- Start by posting your vision on all your internal and external communication and social media outlets. Create and update videos about it.

- Make sure all your managers and executives make it a point to refer to the vision as often as they can, not necessarily repeating it word-for-word, but using different language around it.

- As a leader, express passion about the vision and role model thinking, actions and behaviors to support the vision.

- All managers and leaders in your company must tell each of their employees how they and their job will directly contribute to the vision.

- When making longer-term decisions and developing or updating your goals/objectives, plans, strategies, budgets, resource allocations, programs, projects, hiring and staff promotions and all other activities, leaders and support teams should always consider whether they somehow align with and support your vision.

- Examine and analyze your culture and organizational values and determine what needs to be changed to better support your vision.

- Every time your organization creates a new product or service, opens a new facility, increases R&D, develops innovations in technology, processes, systems, manufacturing or brings about improvements in any area that supports your vision, then broadcast those achievements that actually show the reality of getting closer to your vision.

Omar's Bright Ideas

Summary of How to Make a Difference with Your Vision

1. Your organization should have a vision, preferably in a statement and a full description

2. As a visionary leader, you help create a vision and bring it to life by being a role model supporter. Constantly and energetically remind and rally people to the vision.

3. Every time you and other managers make decisions, new goals, plans, strategies programs or projects, check to see if they align with and support going toward your vision.

4. Make your vision exciting, adventurous, compelling, bold and daring. Who wants to follow a mediocre, toned-down "conservative," and safe-risk-averse one?

5. "Engineer" a shared vision with relevant contributions from a diverse group of people to ensure widespread support.

6. Monitor and analyze business, technology, social, economic, political and other trends that might affect your vision and adapt and modify it as needed.

7. Consider creating and updating (as needed) a powerful multimedia video to describe in vivid images, video, 3D animations, narration and other digital elements what your vision is.

Chapter 11

Leading Creativity and Innovation
Get Ready to Be a "Big Game-Changer"

"Creative thinking is today's most prized, profit-producing possession for any individual, corporation or country. It has the capacity to change you, your business, and the world."
– Robert P. Crawford

If you want to excel and make a difference in today's world where everyone is standing, you must stand out and above, where others are breaking ground, you must break through and where everyone is moving and changing, you've got to go faster and farther in the right directions in the right ways. It pays to be unique, exceptional and excellent. And that's where creativity and innovation will let you mightily and continuously excel and shine. According to an *Adobe Hiring for the Future* study done in 2014, 94 percent of hiring managers say it is important to consider creativity when hiring a job candidate.

Creativity and innovation in business are essential because of the increasingly rapid pace of various facets of major global change and ferocious competition. Steve Jobs said, "Innovation distinguishes between a leader and a follower." Those leaders invite all levels of (including disruptive) innovation, encourage their employees or followers to drop outdated thinking and take balanced risks. A company's ability to innovate — to tap the potentially enormous value-creating ideas of its employees along with those of its strategic partners, customers, suppliers, and other parties — is anything but faddish, as some decreasing number of detractors claim. In fact, innovation has become a core driver of growth, performance, and valuation. No doubt, "Creativity + Innovation + Innovative Leadership + Supportive Culture = Extraordinary Sustained Profits!"

Widespread Research Confirms the Value of Creativity and Innovation

A mountain of surveys, research and statistics just continue to pile up telling the world that creativity and innovation are more vital than ever before. I came across a fascinating survey of Americans by Time Magazine, Microsoft and the Motion Picture Association of America. It surprised me that people value creativity in others more than some other very important traits and behaviors. According to the study, 94 percent of Americans value creativity in other people compared to 93 percent who value intelligence, 92 percent compassion, 89 percent humor, 88 percent ambition and 57 percent who value personal beauty. Over 8 out of 10 (83 percent) people stated that creativity is important in their professional lives. Linkedin Learning stated, "Creativity is the single most important skill in the world."

Even though it was almost a decade ago, the *IBM Global CEO Survey 2010* interviewed over 1,500 CEO's from 60 countries and 33 industries, concluding that creativity is the most important leadership trait for the future. About 60 percent of CEOs polled cited creativity as the most important leadership quality compared to 52 percent for integrity and 35 percent for global thinking. They suggested that "more than rigor, management discipline, integrity or even vision – successfully navigating an increasingly complex world will require creativity."

According to McKinsey, 80 percent of executives say their current business models are at risk, and 84 percent of those surveyed noted that innovation is important to their growth strategy. The *Accenture 2015 US Innovation Survey* tells an almost exact story in that 84 percent of the executives they surveyed considered the future success of their organizations to be very or extremely dependent on innovation (which depends on creativity). And the innovation beat goes on louder and louder every day.

Creativity and Innovation are the great differentiators and equalizers. Together, they are a phenomenal force. In this chapter, I will cover what creativity and innovation are, what benefits they bestow upon those embracing them and some tips on how you can better apply them for superior results in your organization. A smaller company, for example, with a modest budget, but with a die-hard group of dedicated, smart creatives and innovators — who aggressively implement and apply their imaginative ideas, solutions and strategies — can take on and win market share and boost financial performance against much larger, entrenched companies.

"Companies who are more creative are more successful," says Tucker Marion, a director of the Master of Science in Innovation program at Northwestern University. Innovative leadership is the engine and transmission to help accelerate and drive creativity and innovation throughout your company, university, military unit, association, hospital or any other organization in which you are a supervisor, manager or executive.

Making a Difference by Being Different with Ideas and Actions

IBM is famous for its historic slogan "Think." Apple would use and modify (some say "upgrade") that well-known catchphrase. When Steve Jobs returned to Apple in 1996 when it was floundering, and in need of a serious infusion of creativity, excellence and innovative leadership, he wanted to remind the remaining loyal base that new awesome products were on the way and that Apple is charging ahead full speed on a new road. One way to express that was through an impressive advertising campaign that comprised a simple, grammatically slanted slogan, "Think Different" (as opposed to "Think Differently"). It suggested how Apple's culture will be revitalized in ways that will generate new excitement and value in its upcoming offerings and rally employees, customers and stakeholders when morale was low and the company lost its luster and vigor.

While IBM is still an imposing and impressive innovative company, Apple has remained the creative leader in the industry in many ways because it tightly held its practices to that slogan. In 1997, Steve Jobs narrated a commercial that passionately and eloquently encapsulated his feelings about Apple's concept of "thinking different."

"Here's to the crazy ones, the misfits, the rebels, the troublemakers, the round pegs in the square holes... the ones who see things differently — they're not fond of rules. You can quote them, disagree with them, glorify or vilify them, but the only thing you can't do is ignore them because they change things... they push the human race forward, and while some may see them as the crazy ones, we see genius, because the ones who are crazy enough to think that they can change the world, are the ones who do."

Self-motivated, hyper-creative people can do absolute wonders, but some of the best ones can be difficult, or at least frustrating and annoying to manage and work with. They push or ignore boundaries, question current policies, procedures and processes, challenge the status quo, hate red tape and a burdensome bureaucracy. They shove, they pull and can dismiss and disrupt. They call out blatant stupidity, mediocrity, inefficiency and procrastination. They can't fathom how opportunities (blatantly obvious to them) are being missed, ignored or wasted. They raise the bar high for everyone else. Extraordinarily ingenious, creative people are not trying to be a problem or to be difficult on purpose — they just see, think, feel and act differently. They're highly-engaged, driven and want to grab and accelerate the initiative to make a difference. When they're thwarted, they can retreat or fight back.

What is often paradoxical is that leaders and others in their organizations are increasingly calling for hiring more creative people and also trying to encourage current employees to be more imaginative using the overused cliché of "thinking outside the box." Most entrepreneurial and technology-based companies know how to capitalize upon and leverage extraordinary talent. But when staid, traditional, slow-moving and unadventurous organizations try this, problems often develop. Their management, in a well-meaning way, will ask employees to be more creative, to take more risks, to do things differently and "think outside the box" and, unfortunately, when they do, their managers and executives tell them to "get back in the box." Comfortable, deep-seated habits and a resistant, risk-averse culture with its well-worn ways of dealing with situations are quite difficult to change.

Not Everyone Wants In to the New Way

One of the toughest things about innovation is getting people to realize and accept that the way they are thinking and operating just might not be the best at this time. What worked so successfully in the past can no longer be useful, but, instead, might have a diminishing return and actually be counterproductive as new business models, strong competitive inroads and rapid technology changes makes prior operations, actions and strategies ineffective and obsolete.

Those non-engaged, non-creative employees, who have "settled in" coasting along, or perhaps retired comfortably on the job, prefer not to work with these perceived creative malcontents who just want to rock the boat, shake the tree and "fix what ain't broken." These non-engaged don't want to be challenged, have their bars raised or be part of a seemingly risky, unpredictable outcome. They prefer to ignore or banish these creative troublemakers — who want to change things — elsewhere in the organization.

Large numbers, though, of well-intentioned, engaged employees can get on the creativity bandwagon with the right type of M.A.D. Leadership. Given the opportunity by leaders at all levels for them to make a splash with their ideas, these workers will want to exercise their creativity and, still yet play by the rules, be decent team members, cooperate with management and do a better job by being clever and mentally cunning in their approaches and solutions. They may not be "creative superstars," but they'll add value and worth in many impacting ways. The goal for leaders is to get as many of their people to be as creative as possible.

Enormous Value and Benefits of Being Creative and Innovative

Regardless of what type and size of your organization or company, leveraging creativity and innovation have some significant cumulative benefits to it that include:

- Revenues and profits are boosted while costs and wastes are reduced.
- Faster growth, better competitive advantage and market share dominance.
- Promoting short-and long-term security and overall organizational success.
- Employees are more engaged, motivated, encouraged and confident to take more initiative and achieve stellar results.
- Your brand, image, status and reputation are strengthened.
- Employee, customer and other stakeholders' loyalty and commitment are strengthened.
- Improved ability to better attract top talent and retain them.
- Organizational effectiveness, productivity, efficiency, quality and overall excellence and peak performance of operations are continuously improved.
- Greater sense of work satisfaction and achievement in making a difference.
- Many jobs become more challenging, meaningful, enjoyable and even fun.
- Better ability to get needed funding and other resources.

11. LEADING CREATIVITY AND INNOVATION

Definitions and Differences Between Creativity and Innovation

Creativity is about *thinking* and innovation is about *doing*. Creativity is the act and process (called "ideation") of coming up with useful, novel and imaginative ideas, concepts, strategies, approaches or solutions, for example, for anything in one's personal or professional life. Creativity is about seeing the intersection, pattern and value of seemingly unrelated topics or elements and combining them into something new and better. In business or engineering (and other disciplines), creativity is the capacity and capability within individuals or teams to generate mild-to-wild and, therefore, small-to-huge ideas for the fundamental purposes of solving problems, improving various situations and operations and finding and exploiting wide-ranging opportunities. Well-known science fiction author and screenwriter Ray Bradbury sees it this way, "Creativity is a continual surprise."

Innovation is about *doing* —about applying, implementing or commercializing those creative ideas to develop and market something new, different and better. The term "innovation" is from Latin *innovare,* which means "to make new." Innovation relies upon and exploits and capitalizes upon those creative ideas and proposed solutions. Often innovation is about venturing away from familiar ground into uncharted territory. It can also be defined as a market and industry-differentiating change that creates a sustainable competitive advantage in a product, service or business model and that leads to measurable (and often impressive) value creation for any organization.

Done right, continuous innovation creates significant new value in some way and a superior value proposition in one's products, services and business model that can strongly differentiate them from competitors and provide long term security and prosperity. Innovation is a change that creates new or improved capabilities, functionality and performance. Sustained success involves the ability to take ideas and do something positive with them as

Michael Dell puts it in perspective, "Ideas are a commodity. Execution of them is not."

Innovations can be small and cause incremental improvements and advantages or can be disruptive breakthroughs and quantum leaps. A *disruptive* innovation creates a new market and value network and often makes earlier products or technologies obsolete. A disruptive innovation often comes from unexpected places and creates a new product or service or those so much better in ways the market did not expect, by designing for a different set of consumers or users and later by lowering prices, while boosting features and performance. The electric typewriter, for example, replaced the manual one and the word processor and then the computer and printer replaced all those other devices.

The transistor, rockets, television, large computers, jet aircraft, skyscrapers, lasers, electric cars, antibiotics, robotics, personal computers, smartphones are just a few examples of hundreds of major innovations over the last 75 years. A single transistor was demonstrated in December 1947 (essentially making the vacuum tube obsolete) and in 2019 Apple released their A13 chip the size of a fingernail with 8.5 billion transistors on it. That's impressive, continuous innovation! In this case, incremental innovations over the years or decades become disruptive.

These terms for creativity and innovation are often about semantics and context. If you *do* an impressive creative painting or sculpture, is that an "innovation?" No, it's a work of art. If you design, engineer and manufacture a guitar with greater technology (with new features and improved functionality and performance), for example, then that's likely considered an innovation, if even an incremental one. What if you are a fashion designer and bring out a beautiful new design for clothes or shoes. It's not an innovation, but a beautiful new creation. Sometimes it seems one is splitting hairs on the definitions of both.

11. LEADING CREATIVITY AND INNOVATION

Some people, especially those in business, engineering and science prefer using the term "innovative" instead of "creative" because, to them, it has a more perceived sense of practicality, usefulness and gravitas, whereas "creative" to them seems to imply more of an "artistic, perhaps abstract flair" to them, and therefore, more relevant to the arts, entertainment and various design functions. However, both terms can be interchangeable and meaningful in many respects.

I'm sure you've heard the terms "continuous improvement" or "kaizen" a Sino-Japanese word for improvement. Usually, these terms refer to small, incremental improvements in processes, manufacturing and other areas. The Japanese made kaizen famous, for example, when all the employees on an assembly line in an auto plant like at Toyota, launched the *Creative Idea Suggestion System* back in 1951.

Between its inception and 1991 (40 years later), Toyota workers logged over 20 million ideas! Still, Toyota employees generate more than a million process improvement ideas annually, and astoundingly 90 percent of those ideas are implemented. Ever wonder why Toyota is one of the top automakers around the world known for quality and reliability? They mastered how to maximize employee participation and eager engagement. While some companies look for spectacular breakthroughs and quantum leaps in innovations, other companies use thousands or more of small ideas can add up to make a big difference. Yet some companies or organizations (like the military) focus on both — a broad band of ideas ranging from small ones to BIG, game-changing — even industry disruptive — ideas.

In your organization, there are those creative (right-brain) people who can offer up lots of great ideas, solutions and strategies, but may not be the right ones to apply or commercialize them. You also need the left-brain implementor types who thrive on details and have the drive and skill to meticulously plan and then effectively follow it through to make things happen in a timely and successful way.

Traits of Creative People and How They Come Up with Their Ideas

Did you ever wonder how creative you are? You may not realize it just yet, but let me assure you that you are, indeed, creative if you give it a chance. Lots of people who think they might not be hotbeds of ideas discover that their imaginations can erupt once given the chance to do so. Everyone is creative to a degree, some more so. There are those who seem naturally creative, while others need to develop and nurture that skill, which it is. I found that once people build their "thinking muscle," they can become positively addicted to getting and staying on the idea bandwagon that will visibly make a difference on the jobs and in their lives.

Albert Einstein said, "Without creative personalities able to think and judge independently, the upward development of society is as unthinkable as the development of the individual personality without the nourishing soil of the community." Who are these creative individuals and teams whose profound insights spark groundbreaking inventions, technology breakthroughs, unique artistic works and quantum leaps in science, engineering, business and the arts? What special characteristics do they share and how can any of us develop or boost those traits to supercharge our own creativity? Here are just some of the typical traits of those with unfettered imaginations. They...

1. Come Up with Many Ideas Quickly. Imaginative people come up with lots and lots of ideas and they take the initiative to volunteer those ideas. Some are mental race car drivers with their quicksilver imaginations speeding forth with mild-to-wild ideas across the finish line. Granted, most of their ideas will not be blockbusters (and many might be unworkable), but they make a habit of hatching lots of ideas quickly, knowing that even a small percentage will be valuable perhaps with a few blockbusters over time.

2. Are Flexible in Their Thinking Styles. They see and examine situations from a wide spectrum of perspectives, contexts and positions, even dropping prior beliefs, rules and habits in the quest for fundamental breakthroughs in thinking. They are truly 360-degree thinkers and problem-solvers, which is the opposite of narrow-minded ("tunnel") thinking that severely limits the wide, powerful expanse of options, variations or alternatives to an original idea. Imaginative people use "kaleidoscopic" thinking by taking data, situations, phenomena, assumptions, discoveries and insights and then mixing, twisting, shaping or otherwise manipulating them to see dramatically new patterns.

3. See Hidden Relationships and Make Unusual Connections. Creative people have the impressive ability to recognize unusual relationships and make those associations and connections and see things in a different and an original way that others easily miss. An idea or ingenious invention, for example, is usually a new combination of previous elements and the capacity to take those known elements and put them into new, surprising combinations because of seeing relationships.

4. Love Being Creative and Are Intrinsically Motivated. These special people are motivated and exhilarated by the sheer joy and satisfaction of doing something that is new, different and better. They are totally committed and passionate in their work. You don't have to pay them, cajole them or even reward them (though that it appreciated) — just get out of their way, give them support and watch them do amazing things. What demotivates them is repetitious, uninteresting "maintenance work" that is not challenging to their imagination and sense of adventure.

5. Gather and Absorb Diverse Information and Ideas. Creative people always search for and gather information from numerous, wide-ranging (even exotic) sources unrelated to their primary field of work, knowing they will find something of use somewhere and sometime to make that unlikely combination. Many regularly go to arts and crafts stores, the theatre, museums, bookstores, seminars, toy, tool and gadget stores and anyplace that stimulates their senses, emotions and vision. Any source that can generate enlightening ideas and unique experiences for them is welcomed. Some are voracious readers of disparate magazines and publications. They surf unusual web sites and online articles. Then, they piece together what they digest in the cleverest, often brilliant ways.

6. Persist and Persevere and Withstand Withering Criticism and Skepticism. Innovative leaders like Elon Musk, Steve Jobs, Jeff Bezos and creative inventors, entrepreneurs, artists, engineers, scientists, marketers and others have die-hard insulation against self-doubt and criticism from those who think their ideas or solutions are folly, impractical or out-of-bounds. Despite numerous failures, obstacles and setbacks, these hardy visionaries persevere with their strong will and determination. They don't care about the pessimistic opinions of critics or naysayers with their gloomy predictions.

7. "See Things Differently." Creative people are highly observant, and they always have their "antennas" up to spot opportunities others would miss by a mile. Wherever they go, they put their "receivers" on and are always on the lookout for something new and maybe striking they could somehow use. They have extraordinary visual, auditory or kinesthetic mental imagery. Forward-thinking engineers and scientists find that instead of looking for small incremental improvements, they strive to reinvent a process or come up with a fascinating and valuable surprising way of approaching a problem or potential opportunity.

8. Push Themselves to the Limits. Creative people aggressively drive themselves to work at the upper limits of their "competence envelope." They relentlessly push themselves into areas unexplored by others – stretching their mental and emotional abilities to the limit in an (often) unattainable attempt to quench their thirst for new frontiers of knowledge, achievement and extraordinary creation. These are forward-moving "pioneers" (not "settlers or squatters") who often endure long, agonizing hours to smash through barriers and limits others thought inconceivable.

9. Take Risks and Overcome Failures. Creative problem-solvers, inventors and innovators know full well what Charles F. Kettering, head of research at General Motors (1920-1947), engineer, inventor and holder of 186 patents wisely said, "Virtually nothing comes out right the first time. Failures, repeated failures are finger posts on the road to achievement. The only time you don't fail is the last time you try something and it works.

Experienced innovators know that when trying for breakthroughs and quantum leaps, they will experience many, many "learning moments and lessons." Successful innovators take smart, calculated, prudent (sometimes BIG) risks, otherwise their achievements will be limited. While they don't like "failures," they tolerate them and learn and progress from them as they move forward.

10. Are Often Playful and Humorous. Creative people never doubt their imagination, brainpower or inventiveness. Many see themselves as "different" in the way they think and behave. You may hear some complain that "they don't really belong" or fit in with the group at work in a more buttoned-down environment. But, in Google, Apple, Space X, Pixar, IDEO and other cultures they thrive. Without such a supportive climate (especially with the companionship of other creative "soul-mates"), they can feel underutilized and depressed. They are often quite uninhibited in not just their thinking, but sometimes their behavior and this sometimes transfers to their sense of child-like fun and playfulness. Playing and acting silly (within limits), at times, is often a healthy, innocent release for the strenuous mental effort they often expend in their challenging quests to overachieve.

Getting More Creativity from Your Employees or Followers

Leadership is not just about applying your skills, creativity and experiences to the job — it's about bringing out the very best performances in your employees, teams and stakeholders for your organization. I must admit that I love making a difference by getting others to make a difference through their creative ideas, concepts, solutions and anything else. Whether you call it "Servant Leadership" or "Humble Leadership", I conditioned and disciplined myself to acknowledge that I don't have all the answers or even most of them.

So, my primary job, then, is to use my "Transformational Leadership" style to empower, guide and direct my employees to focus on needed change, creative solutions and a dedication to smartly and cost-effectively implement new products and services, advanced technology and the improved processes and systems they envision. Here are some basic but effective ways I've found to get high engagement and abundant ideas from the people I've led over the years:

One: Clarify that you expect, want, need and appreciate lots of ideas. When you, as a supervisor, manager or leader, communicate that you're opening up an "idea factory" and will honor all ideas, it's a good start. Clarify that you want all ideas whether they are small or big ones. Set expectations and explain that you will listen to *all* of them with an open mind with, however, no commitment to use those ideas until they are fairly and carefully vetted. Try to quickly implement as many ideas as you can to encourage a future steady stream.

Two: Plan and communicate your idea needs. Determine what specific issues, problems, areas and projects would best be served by applying creative thinking to them. Then let your people know what those priorities are in which to focus. But, clarify that you want them to generate ideas about anything else that might prove valuable. Along the way, give positive, constructive and specific feedback on how people are doing with their ideas.

Three: Form special teams. Teams are the best to creatively solve problems, develop powerful strategies, and brainstorm ideas for all types of improvements and to brainstorm for new opportunities for your organization. Carefully consider building the team with a mix of dedicated people of various talents, skills, experiences and backgrounds. Name a team leader who has good facilitation skills and give your team some helpful guidelines on how to best operate.

Four: Consider creativity training for both employees and managers. Even a half-day workshop where people can learn impactful techniques to get more and better ideas, how to evaluate them and then learn how to best "sell" them to management can be invaluable. The more the training, the better.

Five: Set up a system to capture, evaluate and prioritize ideas. Make your employees know how to best submit their ideas for review. Create a process and method to gather, sort/categorize and then prioritize ideas for evaluation and possible implementation. Provide guidelines on ideal ways to "package" (describe, explain, justify) ideas. Then establish specific criteria for analysis and evaluation of ideas and determine who (a dedicated person, team or special committee) will then select those ideas for either further consideration or application. Often managers can simply listen to smaller ideas and apply them quickly or pass them on for further investigation.

Six: Recognize, reward and publicize good ideas. Always show appreciation when anyone will volunteer ideas, answers or possible solutions. You can simply recognize and thank a person on the spot, email or text or even a warm, hand-written thank you note. You can publicly recognize individuals or teams in company newsletters, emails or at meetings or larger gatherings. Consider small-to-larger rewards of cash or gift cards, actual gifts, time off work or inviting people to lunch or dinner. Be creative and personalize how you reward those who offer ideas.

Seven: Create a "Special Meeting Room." If your organization has several meeting rooms of adequate size for teams of 7 – 10+ people, you may want to imaginatively design and decorate one of them in ways that will make idea sessions more informal and fun. Large, wall-size whiteboards and supplies of various color markers, sticky notes and projection system for laptops, tablets and phones will facilitate effective sessions. Consider giving the room a catchy name like "Idea Den" or "Imagination Cave" or "Genius Hideout" or whatever one your groups like to use. Overall, if possible, create a brain-friendly workplace that is comfortable, unique and fun.

Eight: Consider Allocating Time for "Special Projects." According to a 2017 Gallup American Workplace Survey, 35 percent of workers are given time to be creative at work only a few times a year. In 1948, 3M introduced a unique program that became one of the signature factors for its innovation reputation. The "15%" program which continues right to today allows employees to use of to six hours a week on their own projects, that cover areas beyond their job responsibilities. They can work their idea and see what becomes of it. Apple has created its own version of Google's "20% time" that gives employees two weeks for special projects. HP and other companies provide sufficient time to be creative. Perhaps your organization can create its own unique copy of that to accelerate your creative projects, experiment and introduce innovations that may flourish.

Starting Innovation or Boosting It in Your Organization

Innovation is bringing imagination into reality — the successful exploitation of new ideas. It can be taught, managed and spurred. Innovation can be a very complex venture and challenging sustainable endeavor depending upon the type and degree of it you are pursuing, or innovation can be a toned-down, more simplified and relatively easy approach and method yielding modest, but worthwhile results. The innovation process can be a messy, chaotic and frustrating series of events, if not planned or implemented properly, especially if your organization is looking for some major quantum leaps in product design, technology, material science, or engineering, for example where failure, after failure happens in the pursuit of radical breakthroughs. If innovation were that straight forward and problem-free, all organizations would embed it throughout their mission, plans and operations.

While some leaders are looking for those game-changing, big and bold disruptive ideas and innovations that will be an explosive in their impact, it pays to initially look for the relatively easy-to-implement ideas that add up to improving your operation. In the following, I'll cover some key highlights about this topic that is so important to leaders today. Though, to do it justice, it really requires reading numerous books, online videos and articles and getting training to understand this complex and often daunting adventure better. Here are initial insights to think about:

- Innovation should come from everyone and anyone in your organization from top-down as well as bottom-up.

- Think "10." If you want incremental change, you might think in terms of improving it by 10 percent. If you want radical, revolutionary change, think 10 times improvement. Adding technology or new or extra equipment to a process, for example, might improve it 10-25 percent, while reinventing the entire process might improve it 100 percent and much more.

- Continuous innovation — a commitment to its systematic practice — is most successful when it has the following" a) Visionary leadership; b) a solid plan and strategy with measurable goals, metrics and risk analysis; c) an effective process that gathers and takes ideas and proposed solutions and turns them into all kinds of innovations; d) a structured organization from top-to-bottom in all departments that drive the innovation process forward; and e) ongoing skills development and training that furthers and strengthens innovation activities and specific projects; and f) a system to recognize, publicize and reward not just accomplishments, but worthy efforts where important learning and progress took place.

- If you're starting or even expanding your innovation activities, do you specifically know what problems need solving or what possible opportunities you seek or what new products, services you want to develop or what new markets you want to open? Your innovation plan/strategy and actions should be closely aligned with your organization's vision, mission and goals to amplify the overall results you want.

- Consider having people who want to be involved with innovation projects take the Kirton Adaption-Innovation Inventory assessment. This valuable tool will help identify where someone is on the scale between "adaptor" or "innovator." This valuable tool shows the level and style of creativity, problem-solving and decision making.

Typical Obstacles and Barriers to Innovation

While creativity and innovation have a multitude of strategic benefits and can deliver superb results, fostering and sustaining creativity and innovation have some major challenges attached to making them eminently successful on a long-term basis. The *15th Global CEO Survey* by PwC in 2012 found that "Overall, one in three CEOs say they are concerned that a skills gap is hampering the ability to innovate. Yet, there are other impediments to getting innovation rocking and rolling. Here are twenty (20) of those that will negatively impact the chances for innovation starting and flourishing. While these "challenges" can seem daunting, once you identify and analyze those that are relevant to your organization, you can explore imaginative ways to minimize or overcome them to move innovation forward for your organization.

- ✓ The biggest obstacle is that one's culture is not conducive for change, innovation and seeking out of exceptional new opportunities. A culture of innovation without creativity is like building a house without the foundation.

- ✓ No organization-wide interest and commitment along with short-term focus and shifting priorities.

- ✓ Prior successes with the belief it is best to continue that way.

- ✓ Inadequate resources, budgets and qualified personnel to handle new projects.

11. LEADING CREATIVITY AND INNOVATION

✓ No effective innovation vision, plan/strategy, system, measurement criteria and detailed process aligned with overall goals and the company's strategic business model.

✓ The organization does not understand how to identify, nurture, manage and develop creative thinking skills from employees and stakeholders.

✓ Procrastinating, being too cautious, overly analytical and risk-averse.

✓ No training, coaching and mentoring for creativity and innovation development.

✓ Lack of ownership and leadership of innovation by the top leaders.

✓ Micromanagement that impedes employee initiative and freedom to experiment and come up with far-reaching ideas.

✓ Suffocating bureaucracy, counterproductive politics, silos and fiefdoms throughout the organization.

✓ Several setbacks during innovation projects that soured management on it.

✓ No formal idea capture system to gather and then select and prioritize best ideas for implementation and no employee recognition and reward system for successful ideas.

✓ Autocratic top management who are the only source for ideas and innovative projects.

✓ Low employee morale and motivation to get involved and excel.

✓ Short, unachievable deadlines and also that employees are already overloaded and overwhelmed with their work assignments. According to Adobe, a whopping 80 percent of US and UK people report they feel pressure to be productive rather than creative at work.

✓ Employees are "punished" (to varying degrees) for trying promising new things that did not pan out as expected. Ideas are criticized prematurely or made fun of by a "devil's advocate" instead of "angel's advocate."

✓ Unrealistic expectations about innovation and its operation and results.

✓ Inability to form strong, diverse teams that will brainstorm great ideas and then implement them effectively and efficiently.

✓ Too long development times for intended innovation projects.

25 Valuable Questions to Assess Creativity and Innovation in Your Organization

Here are detailed questions to help gauge, measure and analyze the areas that impact creativity and innovation in your organization. It's helpful to pass these questions along to a representative sample of others (employees, managers, executives, stakeholders) in your department, division or entire company to get a diverse and more accurate view of the current status. You (or a team) can then analyze the important feedback and look for ways to become better in each area of creativity and innovation.

1. On a scale of 1-10 (10 being tops), how creative and innovative do you think your company is right now? Explain why you scored it that way.

2. Some companies see themselves as an "Idea Factory." In your organization, are the number of ideas that most employees usually propose to management: a) lots of ideas on a regular basis: b) a medium number of ideas; c) or, few or none?

3. What motivates most people to offer up ideas in your company eagerly? What demotivates or prevents people from coming up with and giving lots of new ideas?

4. How would you describe the ideas that generally get a fair hearing within your company: a) all ideas — even those that are wild and far out; b) Ideas that are "practical" and risk-free; c) Ideas that are "low-hanging fruit — ones that are very easily generated and the most obvious?

5. Where do most ideas come from in your company: a) leaders, executives and managers; b) those in R&D, product development, marketing or other "creative functions;" c) from anyone and everyone?

6. On a scale of 1-10, how would you rate your organization's culture in supporting, encouraging, promoting and rewarding lots of creativity and innovation? Why that score? What is missing to make the culture better?

7. Compared to your top 2-3 competitors, how would you compare your organization's culture and utilization of creativity and innovation: a) more innovative than your competitors; b) less so; or c) about the same?

8. Does your company have a structured system and process to collect, analyze, prioritize and suggest the best ideas for implementation? How effective is it toward getting lots of ideas and then creating a viable mechanism to implement them?

9. What "types" of ideas are generally frowned upon by your top and middle management and why? To what degree are people scorned, reprimanded or outright punished for recommending promising ideas that ultimately flop?

10. What percentage of ideas are implemented and how long does it generally take? How are potentially blockbuster ideas evaluated?

11. Does your organization have regularly scheduled idea-generating sessions on a widespread basis within most (or all) all departments?

What have been the positive results? If not, why? What percentage of the people facilitating these sessions have been formerly trained using a structured methodology to get optimum results from teams?

12. Who are the most creative people in your organization and why are they considered so? Overall. how "entrepreneurial" is your organization, and why or why not?

13. What percentage of managers in your organization encourage and support people to come up with ideas to improve operations and financials? Generally, how open-minded are most managers to fresh, new ideas that may be different in nature compared to what has been suggested in the past?

14. Describe what many in your organization might remember as historically important ideas that have changed your organization? When was the last time people can recall an idea considered significant, a breakthrough or a quantum leap in some strategic respect?

15. Do employees in your organization typically jump at the first viable solution to a problem or go on explore (in greater depth) other different solutions that might prove superior to the first one that appeared to work "well enough?"

16. Does your organization have a senior person responsible for promoting and supporting innovation throughout your company? If so, what is the result? If not, why?

17. Do you have any creativity workshops as a part of your training curriculum? If not, why? If so, what are the outcomes from them?

18. What percentage of executives, managers and professionals in influential and strategic positions have been trained to effectively present their ideas, concepts, strategies or proposed solutions? How

would you generally describe the quality of presentations (formal or informal) in your organization: a) very good; b) acceptable; c) mediocre; d) poor and why?

19. On a scale of 1-10, how supportive is your culture and management to calculated risk-taking that might cause superior results? Why do you feel that way?

20. What specific bureaucratic rules, procedures, norms, policies, methods, and management behaviors stifle creativity and innovation? How can they be eliminated, minimized, or modified?

21. What is the breakdown between employees focusing on problem-solving ("fighting fires") and opportunity-seeking (exploring and grabbing new opportunities) for your organization?

22. Do employees feel appreciated for their ideas and recommendations? Do they perceive benefits for being proactive with innovation? What causes employees to stop their flow of ideas and drop out from actively pursuing innovation?

23. Does your organization have a structured innovation process that's regularly used to generate ideas (from mild to wild), prioritize them and then implement the most important ones effectively and efficiently? If so, what is the impact? If not, why?

24. How would you describe the overall communication climate in your organization? To what extent is it open, honest, frank, positive, and supportive versus closed, adversarial, or chain-of-command driven, for example? How does communication affect the way people react to ideas and work together to approve, and implement them?

25. Overall, what would you change to make your organization more conducive to creativity and innovation?

Omar's Bright Ideas

Summary of How to Make A Difference with Creativity and Innovation

1. Realize YOU are creative and can be more so and will contribute to your company.

2. Creativity and innovation have enormous benefits. Are your managers and executives promoting, encouraging, supporting creative ideas and solutions?

3. Create a structured process to gather, analyze and prioritize ideas for implementation.

4. Publicize those innovation "victories" and successes to build more momentum.

5. Learn more about innovation from those companies that have done it well.

6. Supportive leadership at every management level is needed to boost innovation.

7. Don't let minor setbacks, "failures" and being risk-averse limit your innovation.

8. Encourage, recognize and reward creative achievements, however small.

9. Add challenge to work projects that stretch people's abilities and give them a sense of worthy achievement. If you can, make work more fun and playful. Celebrate successes.

10. Both right-brain creatives and visionaries must work with logical, rational left-brain employees who are detailed planners and implementors for best results.

Chapter 12

Attention!
Valuable Lessons We Can Learn from Military Leaders

"What I'm trying to do is teach people how to actually get individuals in organizations to do the kinds of things to make a difference. It starts with not just studying the mechanics, but really understanding how people operate."
– General Stanley A. McChrystal

At ease, readers. In this information-packed chapter, you'll discover fascinating and valuable insights about several military leaders (from the past and present) and how they led — and why they won. You can apply those key principles and proven strategies of theirs in your company or organization, regardless of its size, makeup and mission. When I was younger, I seriously thought of joining the U.S. Marines. I guess fate and other circumstances led me down a different path back then and I did not join. But, I always thought the U.S. military had great leadership learning lessons for people in business, government or other organizations, especially those that go through wrenching change and have need of significant transformation. I think you'll both learn from and enjoy reading these examples and tips on great leadership.

There's a reason a lot of organizations hire experienced military officers and NCOs (Non-Commissioned Officers). They get carefully planned training, educational and experiential events far more expensive, extensive and time-consuming than leadership training in industry, government or elsewhere. Even junior leaders usually hold high levels of authority and responsibility at lower levels in their military units because of this training and development. The core values of duty, respect, loyalty, honor, integrity, service and courage are ingrained in soldiers, and that builds character.

General Mark A. Milley said the traits needed in today's Army leaders include agility, adaptability, flexibility, mental and physical resilience, competence and most importantly character. The same requirement can and should be said of business leaders. Colin Powell, one of America's most popular and admired leaders and statesman, exemplified those traits along with being a visionary, strategist and optimist. He understood what motivated people, and he made a deep commitment of support to them. Powell was deeply respected for his high moral character and moral courage.

Colin Powell's Leadership Style, Principles and Advice

Colin Luther Powell is a highly-decorated retired four-star general and former Secretary of State who served two tours in Vietnam and served as National Security Advisor, Commander of U.S. Army Forces Command and was the first African-American to be the Chairman of the Joint Chiefs of Staff, the highest military position in the Department of Defense. Rather than graduate West Point, he participated in ROTC (Reserve Officers Training Corps) at CCNY (City College of New York) and graduated in June 1958 with a degree in geology while receiving a commission as a second lieutenant at the same time. Powell said he was a "C average student," but noted that he not only liked being in ROTC and learning about leadership, military disciple and other requirements, but he discovered he was very good at it. That desire and initial skill and will to lead, helped accelerate his 35-year military during which time he held a myriad of staff and command positions and oversaw 28 crises, including the 1991 Persian Gulf War. He defined leadership in this way:

"Leadership is the art of accomplishing more than the science of management says is possible. Leadership is all about people… and getting the most out of people. It is about conveying a sense of purpose in a selfless manner and creating conditions of trust while displaying moral and physical courage."

Powell would say, "Being responsible sometimes means pissing people off." He stressed that trying to win a popularity contest is equal to leadership failure or mediocrity because you'll avoid making tough, often unpopular decisions and you'll avoid confronting people who need to be confronted. If no one is angry, disappointed or somehow taken back with what a leader does, then that leader is not pushing hard enough.

When it came to "pushing," Powell made staff performance, fighting complacency and innovative change a top organizational priority. When he defined the new plan or game, he expected everyone to go along with it eagerly. He always advocated that leaders should ensure that the best performers are more satisfied and rewarded than poor performers and leaders need to get rid of non-performers, who damage the morale and effectiveness of an organization.

I'm sure in your career, you've either worked for a manager or know of one who would say, "I don't want to hear of problems. Don't bring me problems!" General Powell knew that strong leaders make themselves approachable and available. He said, "The day soldiers stop bringing you their problems is the day you have stopped leading them." Problems in business don't go away by themselves. If anything, they might get worse in their impact and consequences as time goes on. Smart managers and leaders encourage people to openly tell them of current or impending problems so they can be addressed and solved. At the same time, if appropriate, it's helpful to train people to analyze the problem and suggest potential solutions *before* they come to the manager and simply describe it.

I strive to be approachable right from the beginning. For the last nine years, I personally met every person who has come to work in the Human Resources Departments where I work. This thirty-minute meeting is an opportunity for me to get to know each person we are on-boarding. I tell them at the beginning "this is not an interview; my team is responsible for that. I want to get to know them personally and give you some insights into my leadership style and where we have been and are going as an organization."

M.A.D.* LEADERSHIP

Powell always insisted on massive and decisive action. He stressed that leaders must take the initiative and action without waiting for the official blessing to try out new ideas, strategies, solutions or approaches. Don't pick people who passively wait for marching orders. "You don't know what you can get away with until you try," he would say. That doesn't mean being impulsive or recklessly fighting authority or the bureaucracy. Innovative leadership is all about seeking opportunities that others miss and doing something about it in a proactive way.

The General cautioned other leaders not to be afraid to challenge the pros and the experts, even in their own area of competence and expertise. You can learn from them and seek their advice and information, but don't blindly believe they are infallible and are not subject to being wrong and out of date with their proposed solutions. Powell cautions us to avoid blind obedience to anyone. He said, "Don't be buffaloed by experts" — those who can be intimidating with their resume and accomplishments. Experts often fight change and can be closed-minded to new ideas and approaches. Even fresh-faced budding leaders can have better strategies, concepts and ways to improve things compared to the "old guard" experts.

Another key leadership principle of Powell's is "Perpetual optimism is a force multiplier" as he calls it. In the same manner, broadcaster and playwright Lister Sinclair's quote, "A frightened captain makes a frightened crew" is so true in any situation, especially one where people are anxious, concerned and even scared and panicked. Leaders should display a calm and composed demeanor, like Powell impressively did — "grace under fire." Showing optimism and communicating positive expectations in the face of great adversity is a vital leadership trait and behavior to develop. If a leader exhibits cynicism and pessimism that will have a devastating psychological ripple effect among followers. Masterful leaders have a positive gung ho attitude that uplifts others and gives them the confidence and will to collectively say and believe, "We can change things here. We can make a real difference. We can win!"

12. ATTENTION!

Lewis B. "Chesty" Puller was a U.S. Marine Corps Lieutenant General who served with extraordinary bravery, leadership competence and distinction in World War Two and the Korean War. He is the most decorated Marine in American history and is considered a Marine's Marine. His optimism transmitted to his men was boundless, shown by his famous quote about being encircled by the enemy, "All right, they're on our left, they're on our right, they're in front of us, they're behind us. They can't get away this time." Colin Powell reflected and communicated this same sense of great optimism to all those he came in contact with whether they were "grunts" in the field or his senior generals.

When he started as a junior Second Lieutenant, Powell asked a general how he could become one in his military career. The general answered:

"Son, you've got to work like a dog. You've got to have moral and physical courage. There may be days you're tired, but you must never show fatigue. You'll be afraid, but you can never show fear. You must always be the leader." Powell was excited about this advice and said, "Thank you, sir. So, is this how I become a general?" The general replied, "No... that's how you become a first lieutenant, and then you keep doing it over and over and over." Apparently, Powell took that guidance to heart based upon his meteoric rise in his military and government careers.

In all his dealings, Colin Powell had a very dignified, calm and even-keeled manner. Yet his competence, command presence leadership, quiet strength and great character were evident to anyone to whom he came in contact. Now, let's look at three more military leaders from the past.

Considered to Be the Best "Commander" In History

He was the King of Macedon at only twenty years of age and he built and shaped his army to conquer Persia —the greatest empire on earth at the time. Alexander the Great (356 BC–323 BC) was brilliant and transcendent in many ways, but flawed and controversial (especially later in his life) as well. He was a paragon of a leader who always led from the front as the "human tip of the spear" and whose success has never been equaled, even to this day. Courageous, visionary, bold and daring, he is surely known by experts as the greatest military commanders and generals of all time.

His leadership, strategies and campaigns are still studied and revered among the world's top militaries. He motivated and led a relatively small but supremely skilled army to do the impossible on a regular basis. Alexander inspired his men face-to-face in a personal, not just professional way. He loved, appreciated and rewarded his men, and they, in turn, reciprocated with unbounded love and iron-clad loyalty and fierce performance.

His achievements and victories were spectacular. Alexander left Northern Greece in the spring of 334 B.C. and traveled 22,000 miles in his epic 12-year journey of adventure. Alexander's empire stretched more than 10,000 miles (comprising 1 million square miles) that included modern-day Lebanon, Iran, Iraq, Pakistan, Turkey, Syria, Egypt and a small part of India. Along the way, he founded 70 cities — 20 cities that bore his name, most notably Alexandria in Egypt. In his relatively short (32 years) lifetime, he fought 70 battles, even defeating well-trained armies four and five times the size of his. He never lost one battle because he had much better trained and motivated soldiers, superior creative strategies, innovative weapons, along with his unequaled daring, courageous and brilliant leadership.

His Courage and Risk-Taking Were Legendary

Alexander fought valiantly with his men and was the last great commander to lead from the front — every single time. He suffered 30 wounds with 9 being serious including an arrow shot through his lung, a catapult missile hurled through his shoulder and a serious head injury that almost blinded him. Alexander "walked the talk" with his total willingness to do what he asked of his men. Whether it was strategic planning, manual labor or honing his own skills as a soldier and horseman, he worked harder than those he led. He was enormously respected and admired for that.

12. ATTENTION!

Alexander took calculated risks. He seemingly feared nothing in battle or life. Many of today's executives are afraid to speak their minds, take appropriate risks and do what is right, given even mild opposition. To be an exceptional leader takes courage, a willingness to risk it all (sometimes) and a strength to get in front and lead others when the going gets tough.

Had a Vision Like No Other and Turned It into Reality

Achieving spectacular aims requires thinking really B-I-G and bold. These leaders see far ahead and far above the crowd. They have a strong sense of what can be and what should be. Alexander had an audacious vision of conquest, of greatness, of unprecedented victories. His father, King Phillip II of Macedon (who was killed before his son became king) said to his son, "My boy, you must find a kingdom big enough for your ambition." Alexander dreamed, planned and executed on a grand scale and he frequently communicated his vision so his men would share in it and eagerly commit to it, even under dire hardships and sacrifices.

The visionary leadership aspect is so important because it communicates a sense of exciting, worthwhile purpose to people and, if it's crafted in a compelling and captivating way, it will ignite their emotions and fill their hearts to help achieve it. The chance to make a significant difference and be part of something greater than oneself, whether in any organization or field of work, can be an enormously proud and energizing feeling of accomplishment. When leaders tap into the hopes, dreams and aspirations of their employees, stakeholders or followers, they increase their chance of getting everyone on board with the vision. Well-known leadership author and expert Warren Bennis said, "Leadership is the capacity to translate vision into reality." Alexander did not just see the future as make it happen.

Undaunted and Unstoppable Was His Style and Personality.

Alexander tried to convince the Phoenician island of Tyre to submit to his authority in 333 B.C. They refused, knowing that to stage an invasion, ocean warfare was not one of Alexander's strengths. The Phoenicians were the world's best sailors at the time. They felt a sense of invincibility by great defenses, a seagoing armada and being surrounded by water. Undaunted, Alexander had his innovative corps of engineers build an impressive causeway 2,000 feet long and 200 feet wide from the mainland to the island. They took seven arduous months, laboring under extremely adverse conditions, including constant, withering enemy fire to build it. He made sure he achieved his objective he wanted with a minimal loss to his forces. Alexander took Tyre. That further built his "eliteness," credibility and unwavering loyalty from his troops.

He Motivated and Inspired His Troops to "Regular Peak Performance"

How do you get men to march 30 miles a day every day in the searing desert heat or brave frigid cold going over 15,000-foot peak mountains while dealing with other near-debilitating hardships? In the spring of 329 B.C., Alexander led his starving, frigid, snow-blinded troops (many of who were more than 60 years old) across the treacherous and icy Hindu Kush mountain range in central Asia, a feat of amazing endurance that historians agree to this day far surpassed even Hannibal's impressive crossing of the Alps. It takes a beloved, respected and trusted leader to inspire and galvanize them to go where they feel they cannot go any more.

Prior to each of his meticulously-planned battles, Alexander reviewed his troops, conversed with officers on strategy and assured them of victory. He singled out soldiers who had performed bravely in battles and praised their exploits with the understanding that they will, again prevail. He's said to have remembered the names of hundreds of men. Alexander tolerated no half-hearted efforts from his followers and troops. As such, they felt they were the fortunate elite and blessed to be with the Great Alexander if a battle was to ensue.

Was "One" With His Followers

In today's business world, too many executives separate themselves from their employees in their expensive "ivory towers." They have their impressive, expensive offices, private dining rooms and even exclusive elevators to avoid contact with the "commoners." Exorbitant salaries plus bonuses and benefits, along with getting tens of millions from a golden parachute will not engender loyalty from employees being outsourced, let go or having their salaries frozen and benefits downgraded. Not Alexander! He always vigorously and extensively trained right along with his troops. He ate what they ate and if water was in short supply, he drank what they drank. And if their horses were injured or dead, he would dismount and walk with them.

Alexander saw his whole undertaking as a team effort. He never placed himself too highly above his men. Alexander never flinched at enduring hardships, together with his troops. He was always closely fighting, celebrating, governing (conquered territories) and sharing in the glory with them. He bonded with his troops as few great generals ever did and they loved him for it.

Exceptional executives and other organizational leaders spend the time and effort to get to know their people (not just their high-level reports), visit their various offices and facilities, and genuinely demonstrate that they will sacrifice, if necessary, along with others. Whether you call it 'Management by Walking Around," they become more visible and approachable either in person, via emails, texts or other media. Apple's Steve Jobs was known to answer emails from his employees personally.

Imagine today's executives taking a serious pay cut when times are tough, and employees are expected to unduly sacrifice alone. How do employees feel when their jobs are being outsourced (or their salaries frozen or cut) and the big shots at the top are getting giant bonuses and outrageous golden parachutes, sometimes even when their failed leadership caused their organizations to be at risk or outright fail?

Supreme Strategist and Unsurpassed in Its Seemingly Flawless Execution

Alexander was a brilliant strategist who meticulously studied military history and campaigns and learned tactics firsthand by observing his father, Phillip II of Macedon. As an innovative leader, he relied on extensive intelligence gathering, competitive analysis of his enemies and systematic, and creative planning to enable him to develop a complete and imaginative range of options that would optimize his strategy depending upon the situation and environment.

Alexander was a master at precisely and optimally coordinating all parts of his military machine including his deft deployment of his superb cavalry and the renowned, impenetrable Macedonian phalanx (that used a *sariss* — a spear that was an 18 ft long sharp pike). In his maneuvers, he was unequaled in his adaptability and surprise that he executed with swift dexterity and mastery. What makes all this so impressive is that Alexander built his empire with an army that numbered only about 40,000 men. This means he had to employ and maneuver his forces to overcome the overwhelming numbers of enemy troops often 3 to 5 or more times larger than opposed him.

Remember that he fought 70 battles, never losing a single one! Great leadership, planning and strategy, innovative weapons, constant training of troops and a well-oiled logistical and supply train—effectively feeding them resources—made all the difference in this warrior-king being outlandishly victorious. He summed up his philosophy of leadership with, "I am not afraid of an army of lions led by a sheep. I am afraid of an army of sheep led by a lion."

12. ATTENTION!

Alexander Listened, Recognized and Richly Rewarded His Troops

"I believe that you should praise people whenever you can. It causes them to respond as a thirsty plant responds to water," said Mary Kay Ash, founder of Mary Kay Cosmetics. She added, "Pretend that every single person you meet has a sign around his or her neck that says, 'Make me feel important.'" Alexander not only made his troops, support personnel and followers feel important, he also made them feel special and elite.

After reach battle, Alexander would go to the troops who were injured and raptly listen to their "exploits of courage and performance," which were often embellished to impress Alexander. He enthusiastically listened and encouraged them to tell him how they bravely conducted the battle, how they vanquished the enemy and how Alexander should be so proud of them. He was an empathic listener who expressed concern for their fatigue, their wounds and their problems. He expounded upon how daunting and daring they were. In front of others, Alexander singled out those worthy of excellence while telling of their fearless fighting and sacrifice. William Shakespeare said, "When the lion fawns upon the lamb, the lamb will never cease to follow him." Though Alexander's troops were no lambs, his special and emotionally affecting treatment of them and how he honored them made them follow him anywhere, regardless of the dangers, hardships and pains.

His troops richly received the bounty of victory together with Alexander. He made sure they were generously taken care of. In today's business world where executives receive disproportionate rewards versus employees, Alexander would have no part of that. How can you maintain loyalty, devotion and fellowship if people feel taken advantage of?

Creativity, Surprise and Ingenuity Works Wonders!

Successful organization executives, along with government, military and political leaders, for example, know that implementing consistent, predicable strategies and actions can make their organization vulnerable when it comes to competitors or other threats. Being smartly unpredictable can knock your competitors off their game. In his 70 winning battles, Alexander, as an innovative leader, *never* fought each one the same way. In military parlance and history, that's unheard of! His creativity and the element of surprise made him so unequalled and successful. Each imaginative strategy was tailored for the terrain, the situation and the type of enemy and leader.

Regarding surprise, for example, in the Battle of Hydapses, he would march his troops every night along the banks of the Hydapses River and order them to loudly blow their trumpets and scream their war cries to arouse and provoke his enemy Porous into action. So, naturally every evening, Porous prepared his men for battle only to witness Alexander's troops beat a hasty retreat, thinking they were afraid or hesitant. This clever charade kept up for days until Porous thought they were bluffing or playing foolish games. Then, Alexander stole across shore near Porous's camp and took swift victory. Creative improvisation was a hallmark of this innovative leader. He used guile, ingenuity and lateral thinking to defeat vastly superior forces with minimal casualties.

Alexander died (mysteriously) at age 32. While he could be generous, compassionate and magnanimous, in his later years, he could be vindictive, murderous and extraordinarily violent, especially after his increasingly drunken outbursts. Alexander's healthy ego and supreme confidence increasingly changed into facets of megalomania, and he began to lose functioning of his prior sterling traits, behaviors and principles. But history still extols him, overall, as bigger than life in so many ways and myth paints him as a demigod and mystical leader.

Dwight D. Eisenhower: An Extraordinary, All-Around Leader

William Shakespeare must have looked in his crystal ball and saw World War Two when he said, "Some are born great, some achieve greatness, and some have greatness thrust upon them." Were it not for that catastrophically deadly event in history, generals (on both sides of the war) would have remained practically nameless, and their innate and powerful leadership abilities and greatness would not have been demonstrated. How do you lead men into the largest and greatest amphibious invasion in history? Clue: you can't lead from behind a desk.

General Dwight David (known as "Ike") Eisenhower was the Supreme Allied Commander during World War II and responsible for the invasion of Europe. The World War II invasion of Normandy, France (commonly known as D-Day) on June 6, 1944, was a massive undertaking to begin to free the European countries from German occupation and take the war straight to Berlin. While the Germans were losing battles, their war was not lost and the fate of the free world was still in serious jeopardy. This invasion was so critical, so complex and so monumental there was a serious risk it might fail if things did not go as meticulously planned. The allies were to land on five beaches codenamed, Omaha, Utah, Gold, Juno and Sword. To put the size and scope of this unprecedented military campaign in perspective, here are some staggering numbers (rounded off):

- 11,500 aircraft involved in the invasion along with almost 7,000 naval vessels.

- On the first day of the landing, over 150,000 men came on land.

- Within five days, over 350,000 men were ashore along with 54,000 vehicles and over 104,000 tons of supplies, material and equipment.

- By June 30th 850,000 men were in France, almost 150,000 vehicles and over 570,000 tons of supplies were unloaded.

If you were General Eisenhower, the Supreme Allied Commander responsible for the success of D-Day, wouldn't you spend all your precious time in the war room with your top generals and admirals to plan, strategize, explore options and critical contingency approaches to ensure that nothing was hopefully left to chance with "Operation Overlord?" The logistics and coordination (with the previous numbers), alone made administration and planning a head-dizzying top priority.

That's *not* what General Eisenhower did. He did not lock himself up in a war room or behind a desk months prior to the Normandy landing. No doubt he spent a great deal of time with the allies going through all possible plans and an overall roadmap for success, knowing they were as well done as they possibly could be. Eisenhower was wise and experienced enough to know that victories are not achieved in rooms by groups of high-level officers, but on the various battlefields where men's confidence, courage, perseverance and will to win was utmost. These men had to push past fear, hardships, pain and suffering and be willing, if necessary, to sacrifice all and die to begin to take an overwhelming victory against a fierce, extremely competent and determined enemy to end this brutal war.

Instead, four months before the world saw the greatest amphibious assault in history with the largest air and sea armada ever assembled, Eisenhower visited 26 Divisions, 24 airfields, 5 warships and numerous military bases, hospitals, depots and other outfits. He wanted to meet and greet as many of the soldiers, sailors and airmen as he could in person, face-to-face. When he arrived at the camp, airfield or other military installation, rather than talk to them in a formal formation, he would ask them to break rank and circle closely around him. Instead of asking them about their training or weapons, as most generals would have done, he would ask them about their families, where they were from, what they wanted to do when the war was over and what life was like back in their home states. By being warm, informal, and approachable, Eisenhower wanted to project that while he was their commander, he was also simply "one of them" on the same mission.

Ike had a genuine tenderness he felt for his men. He gave them encouragement, support and built their confidence and morale. He told them how vital their mission was and told them he would provide as many resources, equipment and weapons to be victorious. When their Supreme Allied

12. ATTENTION!

Commander saw them, shook their hands, and patted them on their backs, he lifted their spirits and helped to stiffen their spines and warm their hearts in a way that demonstrated he truly cared for their individual welfare and success in battle. Eisenhower made sure all of his senior officers followed his lead in visiting thousands of troops to boost their morale and motivation.

Great leaders love being with, getting to know and mingling with the people they lead. Eisenhower once remarked, "In the Army, whenever I became fed up with meetings, protocol and paperwork, I could rehabilitate myself by a visit with the troops. Among them, talking to each other as individuals, and listening to each other's stories, I was refreshed and could return to headquarters reassured that, hidden behind administrative entanglements, the military was an enterprise manned by human beings."

During his frequent visits to the battlefront, Eisenhower saw first-hand the challenging conditions his men were living and fighting under. Rather than hear about it, he experienced it and that helped him to assess the situation and remedy any problems personally. That's why corporate or other leaders need to get out and see, hear, feel and experience firsthand what is happening throughout their organizations

General Eisenhower combined traits and behaviors perfectly suited to the job. He was astute, diplomatic, tactful and highly aware of the political sensitivities of dealing with allied politicians and top military commanders, some of whom were highly opinionated, close-minded, arrogant and self-aggrandizing prima donnas. Those who knew Ike well would describe him as being eminently principled and trustworthy — always shooting straight with them and being trusted to hold their confidences and make the right decisions after consulting with them. His humility and down-to-earth approachability created a feeling of friendship and comfort in others when expressing themselves. That won him the respect, admiration and loyalty of those who served both under and over him during his career.

A lesson we can all learn from this consummate leader is to understand the people who work for you. You must take care of them because not only is it the right and moral thing to do, but also because your success depends upon their performance and accomplishments. He would tell his subordinates that morale can be destroyed by favoritism, neglect, or injustice. It's been said that whatever a leader feels and outwardly shows affects those around him or her.

A leader, therefore, must always strive to be calm, optimistic and positive, especially in times of challenging change, adverse conditions and overall tough situations. Eisenhower told his junior officers, "Optimism and pessimism are infectious and they spread more rapidly from the head downward than in the other direction. Throughout my leadership journey, I've tried to make sure that my highs are never too high, and my lows are never too low.

Omar's Bright Ideas
Summary for You to Make a Difference by Learning from Military leaders

1. Be creative and unconventional in your thinking and plans when needed

2. Craft and communicate a vision and mission that excites and galvanizes your people

3. Motivate, inspire, encourage and take care of your employees or followers

4. Even when you get to the top, be humble, accessible and approachable to all employees

5. Don't try to win a popularity contest with safe decisions or actions that are mediocre.

6. Surround yourself with talented, ethical, and highly competent people best able and driven to support your goals and plans

7. Develop and display the courage to do the right things

8. Maintain self-control to remain calm and composed during tough situations that test your mettle.

12. ATTENTION!

9. Role model the traits and behaviors you wish others to follow.

10. Reward people for results and let go of non-performers who refuse to meet your expectations.

M.A.D.* LEADERSHIP

Acknowledgments

I would like to acknowledge the following people who have Made A Difference in My Life. Ray Anthony for your wisdom and guidance. This would not have been possible without your help.

To Pastor William A. Lawson, Pastor Marcus D. Cosby, Carter D. Womack and Norma Lemon-Turner for all your incredible inspiration and support. In Memory of these two people who passed in 2019 Laura Royball and Kelley Shreck who were dear friends.

To UPS, a great company, that taught me so much about leadership, quality and excellence. And my special thanks to Rick Winters, Spring Williams, Randy Chambers, Charlie Brooks, Myron Gray, Craig Wiltz, Robert Mills, Gwen Lusk, Lee Small, James Buchanan, Jim Collins, Steve Johns, Abdula (Mo) Abdulla, Guy Cemino, Linda Adam. Jay Armistead, Michael Cramer, Felton, Kevan Brewster, Daryl Banks, Tina Baylor, Pat Cassity, Yolanda Clopton, Clarzell Gylliean, Mario Cuellar, Aaron Dallas, George Davilla, Rodney Edwards, Roger Elmessan, Martha Escondon, Kurt Fahrenthold, Michael Fisher, Vincent Gentile, Lenora Gilmore, Meko George, Tony Graves, Marcus Hackett, Polly Hardy, Carl Harris, Steve Holland, Richard Lamb, Mike Leach, Mike Lee, John Liddle, Regina McCowan, Jerome Powell, Thomas Pratt, Marvin President, Angie Rasheed-Stephens, Kyle Shumaker, Mike Simms, Sharon Silvy, Santos Vasquez, and Steve Ward, for their friendship, encouragement and warm support.

When I worked at The City of Houston, there were special people whose teamwork made a real difference in my HR group. They include Mayor Annise Parker, Mayor Sylvester Turner Council Member Wanda Adams, Council Member Dwight Boykins, Ramiro Cano, Jane Cheeks, Waynette Chen, State Representative Garnet Coleman, Mario Dias Eric Dargan, Council Member Jerry Davis, Council Member Amanda Edwards, Commissioner Rodney Ellis, Attorney David Feldman, Chief Rick Flannigan, Alisa Franklin-Brocks,

M.A.D.* LEADERSHIP

Controller Ronald Green, Council Member Larry Green, Nicole Hare-Everline, Harry Hayes, Melvin Hughes, Ray Hunt, Cheryl Johnson, Council Member Jolanda Jones, Velma Laws, Lance Lyttle, Senator Borris Miles, Scott Minnix, Donna Mitchell, Sherry Moose, Alfred Moran, Rod (Godfather) Newman, William Paul-Thomas, Eric Potts, Linda Porter, Dorothy Roaches, Council Member Jack Christie, Council Member Stephen Costello, Bryan Sky Eagle, William Joe Turner, Dr. Modeane Walker, Gerrie Walker, Stacia Washington, Dr. Stephen Williams, Carlecia Wright, Dr. Michael Adams, Burt Allen, Preston Allen, Ted Andrews, Linda Brewster, Anthony Austin, Dr. Rondell Bailey, Pat Bradshaw, Paxton Baker, Allison Bashir, Vanessa Sampson, Dr. Cleveland Black, Dr. Zenglo Chen, Cynthia Briggs, Dr. Ericka Brown, Milton Carroll, Dr. Rhonda Cole, Willie (Bo Will) Davis, Lisa Descant, Tina Esque, Cathryn Cabor, Dr. Bill Flores, Ricky Georgetown, Miguel Gonzales, Eric Goodie, Rhonda Grant, Marvin Hamilton, Arquella Hargrove, Michael Helm, Brian Hicks, Vanessa Henderickson, Michelle Hunnicutt, Leonard James, Jody Jiles, Preston Johnson, Executive Pastor Alexander Johnson, Vernita Harris, Dr. Annette Howard, Reggie Howard, Mike Kahn, Karen Kauffman, Richelle Khalaf, James Koski, Mike Koehler, Tony Lin, Diane Maben, Debbie Maynor, Stephanie Lee, Rene Logans, Keith Manis, Gary Marsh, George Masi, Carl McGowan, Mike McKee, Derrick Mitchell, Rev.David Moore, Eric Mullins, Durce Muhammad, Mark Netoskie, Orlando Ashford, Dr. Ron Parris, Reggie & Alisa Peppers, Larry Perkins, Dr.Eric Peterson, Lashonda Ramming, Eric Rhodes, Judson Robinson, Vanessa Sampson, Gerry Sargent, Phil Searle, Muddassir Siddqi, Harleen Smith, Rhonda Smith, Anthony Snipes, Karun Sreerama, Jackie Stewart, Nicole Streeter, Elliot Susseles, Shawn Taylor, Robert Thomas, Dr. Doug TeDuits, Annika Tycer, Tracey Kearny, Tom Valley, Mark Washington, Linda Thomas, Reggie White, Sherry Williams, Chevelle Wilson, Pricilla Wilson, Theo Woodard, Reggie King, Johanna Wolf and Kari Jo Zika

All of these incredible people helped me be the strong leader I am today, and I stand on the shoulders of giants! Thank you and God Bless you all!

Omar Reid Biography

Omar C. Reid is the Senior Vice President of the Human Resources Department at Harris Health System, also known as Harris County Hospital District. Harris Health System is the 4th largest community-based Hospital System in the United States, which houses a Level One and Level Three Trauma Hospital and 43 Ambulatory Care locations. With over 8,000 employees in the organization, Omar is currently responsible for all Human Resources programs, policies and initiatives, including Talent Acquisition, Organizational Development, Employee & Labor Relations, Compensation, Benefits, and HRIS.

Mr. Reid has an extensive background, which includes six years as the HR Director at the City of Houston, where he was responsible for citywide Human Resources responsibilities and over 25 years with United Parcel Service (UPS) in various operational and administrative capacities. He earned his Bachelor's Degree in Business Administration from the University of Houston – Downtown and his MBA from Texas Southern University. Mr. Reid is a published author of *The Traffic of Life: Characteristics of Effective Leadership*.

He is also a nationally recognized dynamic speaker on leadership, transformation and change. Since 2015, Mr. Reid has served as a member of the Board of Directors for Communities in Schools of Houston, including participation on the Executive Board, Finance, Compensation, Audit and Search Committees. He has a "people come first" personal philosophy and style of leadership. He and his wife, Janice, have a daughter, Briana, who follows the same examples of hard work in education and sports that are exhibited by her parents.

Made in the USA
Coppell, TX
12 February 2021

50248015R00142